HIVE MIND

HIVE MIND

How Your Nation's IQ Matters
So Much More Than Your Own

Garett Jones

STANFORD ECONOMICS AND FINANCE
An Imprint of Stanford University Press • Stanford, California

Stanford University Press
Stanford, California

©2016 by the Board of Trustees of the Leland Stanford Junior University. All rights reserved.

No part of this book may be reproduced or transmitted in any form or by any means, electronic or mechanical, including photocopying and recording, or in any information storage or retrieval system without the prior written permission of Stanford University Press.

Special discounts for bulk quantities of titles in the Stanford Economics and Finance imprint are available to corporations, professional associations, and other organizations. For details and discount information, contact the special sales department of Stanford University Press. Tel: (650) 736-1782, Fax: (650) 736-1784

Printed in the United States of America on acid-free, archival-quality paper

Library of Congress Cataloging-in-Publication Data

Jones, Garett, author.
 Hive mind : how your nation's IQ matters so much more than your own / Garett Jones.
     pages cm
 Includes bibliographical references and index.
 ISBN 978-0-8047-8596-9 (cloth : alk. paper)
 1. Intelligence levels--Economic aspects. 2. Intelligence levels--Political aspects. I. Title.
 BF431.J596 2015
 153.9--dc23
                              2015021620

 ISBN 978-0-8047-9705-4 (electronic)

Designed by Bruce Lundquist

Typeset at Stanford University Press in 11.75/16 Baskerville

"The area which I am about to enter is one that excites a great deal of emotional feeling; nevertheless it is worth examining."
GORDON TULLOCK, "THE ROOTS OF CONFLICT"

CONTENTS

Figures	ix
Acknowledgments	xi
Introduction: The Paradox of IQ	1
1. Just a Test Score?	15
2. A da Vinci Effect for Nations	35
3. James Flynn and the Quest to Raise Global IQ	49
4. Will the Intelligent Inherit the Earth?	65
5. Smarter Groups Are More Cooperative	85
6. Patience and Cooperation as Ingredients for Good Politics	103
7. Informed Voters and the Question of Epistocracy	121
8. The O-Ring Theory of Teams	139
9. The Endless Quest for Substitutes and the Economic Benefits of Immigration	153
10. Poem and Conclusion	165
Data Appendix	169
Notes	171
Bibliography	181
Index	191

FIGURES

Figure I.1: Average cognitive ability estimated in 2009 from earlier PISA, TIMSS, and PIRLS international exams and estimated 2005 GDP per person   9

Figure 1.1: A problem similar to those on the Raven's Progressive Matrices   21

Figure 2.1: National average cognitive ability estimated from PISA, TIMSS, and PIRLS exams compared with national average IQ estimates   47

Figure 4.1: Estimated national average IQ and estimated national savings rates   72

Figure 6.1: Estimated national average IQ and 2014 Corruption Perceptions Index   117

ACKNOWLEDGMENTS

Without the expertise of my childhood friend, psychologist W. Joel Schneider, this book would not exist. A few years after finishing some work on how the Federal Reserve influences short-term interest rates, I was casting about for a new research direction. Joel mentioned that a new dataset had just been created, the first large one of its kind, one that assembled IQ tests from around the world to create rough estimates of something called "national average IQ" for dozens of countries. The authors had run some preliminary statistical tests showing that these test scores predicted a nation's economic performance. Joel suggested that since economists were experts at cross-country economic comparisons and psychologists were experts at IQ testing perhaps there was room for us to collaborate on a project that would address the following question: Were these test scores really robust predictors of national economic performance, or did the results fade away if we tried more rigorous statistical methods? That question led us to coauthor two journal articles, published in the *Journal of Economic Growth* and *Economic Inquiry*. Those articles documented the paradox of IQ; this book is an attempt to resolve that paradox by spelling out the channels of the hive mind.

I've been fortunate to have excellent coauthors on my other IQ-related papers: Omar al-Ubaydli, John Nye, Niklas Potrafke, and Jaap Weel have all been the high-productivity team members one hopes for. I owe a particular debt to my coauthor Rik Hafer, my department chair at my first academic position, Southern Illinois University Edwardsville. Rik has supported my research and my career in ways I cannot repay, and SIUE itself offered generous financial support to my research at critical early stages.

I'm grateful to audiences and discussants at the Latin American Meetings of the Econometric Society, the Asian Development Bank, the Inter-American Development Bank, the Econometric Society World Congress, the University of California San Diego, the University of Missouri, George Mason University, the University of Konstanz, and the Stockholm School of Economics in Riga, and to other audiences that have provided welcome feedback on much of the research underlying this book.

George Mason University's economics department, my new academic home, is surely among the best places in the world to be a social scientist, to ask big, interdisciplinary questions that don't fit neatly into one box. I appreciate my colleagues' trust over the past eight years, and gratefully acknowledge the financial support I've received both from the department and from GMU itself. I offer particular thanks to my chairman, Dan Houser, for helping to arrange course reductions that gave me the opportunity to focus on my research and for doing the largely thankless work of managing that most unmanageable of things, a university department.

I am enormously grateful to Matt Devries and Karen Johnson, who each read the entire manuscript and were my sounding board for early drafts. I also want to thank my colleagues at George Mason University's Center for Study of Public Choice, who discussed ideas and read chapters and offered excellent advice, much of it unheeded: Bryan Caplan, Tyler Cowen, Robin Hanson, John Nye, and Alex Tabarrok. The Center for Study of Public Choice, founded by my late colleague, the Nobel laureate James Buchanan, is that rare place in modern social science, a place of genuine disagreement and debate, where important ideas from across and even outside the political spectrum are evaluated with vigor and civility and human warmth. And my editor at Stanford University Press, Margo Beth Fleming, provided the combination of professional writing advice, intellectual encouragement, and skill at navigating the publication process that academic authors can usually only dream of. If my fellow economists aren't submitting their book proposals to Fleming, they're making a mistake. James Holt and Emily Smith at Stanford and my copyeditor David Horne were also extremely helpful, and Jane Perry proofread the entire text. Finally, I owe everything to my mother and to my late father, who both raised me according to a central truth: that deep down, all human beings are essentially the same.

Obviously, the usual disclaimer applies: all of the remaining errors that exist in this book are my own responsibility.

HIVE MIND

Introduction

THE PARADOX OF IQ

THIS ISN'T A BOOK ABOUT HOW TO RAISE IQ: it's a book about the benefits of raising IQ. And a higher IQ helps in ways you might not have realized: on average, people who do better on standardized tests are more patient, are more cooperative, and have better memories. But while dozens of studies by psychologists and economists have established these links, few researchers have connected the dots to ask what this means for entire nations. And since average test scores vary across nations—whether we're talking about math tests, literacy tests, or IQ tests—an overall rise in national test scores likely means a rise in the number of more patient, more cooperative, and better-informed citizens. This in turn means that higher national test scores will probably matter in ways too big to ignore. And if education researchers and public health officials can find reliable ways to raise national test scores, productivity and prosperity will rise where poverty and disease now flourish.

You can get a sense of how big these effects are by looking across countries: nations that do the best on standardized tests—nations such as Singapore and Finland—usually have governments that are reasonably free of corruption; have decent roads and bridges; and have plenty of private investment in office buildings, factories, and homes. China does well on standardized tests, and particularly in the post-Mao decades, the nation's economy has grown rapidly. The high test scores in these countries are a sign that their citizens have the cognitive skills, the human capital, to take on the complexity of a modern economy.

By contrast, nations where test scores are average or lower tend to be the kinds of places where people have to bribe government bureaucrats to get things done, whether it's the school principal, the bureaucrat at the driver's license office, or the congressman's brother-in-law. And even if you don't have to bribe the government, it's a good bet that the government will be inefficient, sluggish, less than competent. Nations with lower average test scores are usually tough places to take on complex, costly private investment projects, since skilled workers and twenty-four-hour-a-day electricity are hard to come by. Lower-scoring nations aren't places that appeal to international investors, and so private investment tends to drift away. The long-run result of lower test scores? It's often a mixture of rickety bridges, decrepit buildings, slower Internet connections, and less prosperity. On average, nations with test scores in the bottom 10 percent worldwide are only about one-eighth as rich and productive as nations with scores in the top 10 percent.

Outside of a few countries with abundant natural resources, the most important productive asset in each nation is the human mind. And while standardized tests can't tell us everything about how productive the mind is, the tests can tell us more than you might think. Boosting broad mental skills boosts a nation's prosperity, and while standardized tests are obviously not perfect—no statistic ever is—they are a good way to measure those skills.

Think Win-Win

One of Professor Steven Covey's "seven habits of highly effective people" was "Think Win-Win." In the Covey view, a key to success in business and in life is to look for ways to find pie-growing solutions rather than to just focus on grabbing the biggest slice of a fixed pie.[1] Pie-grabbing and pie-growing are both rational actions—they both make you better off, at least in the short run—but nations where people tend to grow the pie will have more pie to eat. So what predicts pie-growing skill? Researchers at Vanderbilt University ran two experiments to find out. One study looked at what traits predicted skill in haggling over the price of an industrial commodity—so one student is "selling" tin for as much as possible to another student who is "buying" the tin for as little as possible.[2] This was a simple pie-slicing game. The researchers collected data on personality as well as scores on the business school General Management Admissions Test, or GMAT, a test that's much like the SAT and similar to some IQ tests.

The second Vanderbilt study put two students into a free-form negotiation game: a mall developer haggling with a potential anchor store (like a Macy's or a Bloomingdale's) over the details of the contract. The second bargaining situation was more multifaceted, more "integrative," as management professors like to say. Could the anchor store sublease space to cosmetics companies? Could it keep different hours than the rest of the mall? Could it sell the same products as other big stores in the mall? Who pays for the escalator? Issues such as those were addressed, along with the usual haggling over the price. Clearly the second study was more complicated than the first. And one thing that IQ-type tests predict is the ability to handle complexity, to keep multiple facts in mind.

So did test scores matter or didn't they? As so often in the study of humans, the answer is "it depends." Student test scores didn't help at all to predict haggling skill in the first, simpler study: students with higher GMAT scores weren't better than others at buying low or at selling high. But in the complicated mall negotiation study, it turned out that the *average* test scores of the pair of players did a moderately good job of predicting success. Pairs with high average

GMAT test scores were more likely to increase the overall value of the project by getting the details of the contract right, and they were less likely to overlook ways to build overall value: they were more integrative. But what about personality traits, how much did they matter for success? The personality measures used in the study—extraversion, conscientiousness, and the rest—all did a worse job of predicting pie-growing behavior than the GMAT score.

On average the high-scoring pairs tended to be pie growers. Other psychology and economic experiments have backed up this basic finding: players with higher scores on IQ-type tests are more likely to take the pie-growing approach, especially in complex situations. One might imagine what that could mean for entire nations.

Your IQ Doesn't Matter That Much

But if test scores matter a lot for nations—a claim that economists and psychologists alike have made in recent years—then we're left with a puzzle. I'm sure you know a lot of people who are big successes in life—people with good jobs and nice kids—who don't do well on standardized tests. I know people like that too. And we both know people who are failures—bad habits, constant legal troubles, no money—who do great on IQ-style tests. And these aren't just one-in-a-million cases: every day we meet smart people with no money and we meet slow learners with good jobs. At the individual level, test scores just aren't a great predictor of success in life.

Economists have known this fact for decades: when it comes to the link between test scores and wages, exceptions are the rule and the link is moderate at best. So knowing a person's IQ—or her SAT score, or how well she does on vocabulary tests—just doesn't tell you all that much about how much money that person earns. Later, we'll have plenty of opportunity to survey what IQ means (it's short for "intelligence quotient") and what it doesn't mean, and we'll survey some of the imperfect techniques used to measure it.

We'll also see that people with higher IQs tend to be taller, quicker to react to a flashing light, and more patient. But for now, consider this one fact: your own, individual IQ score isn't that good at predicting how much you'll earn over the course of your life.

That fact is half of what this book is about, and I've covered it in two paragraphs. Now set that next to another fact—that nations with the highest test scores are about eight times more prosperous than nations with the lowest scores—and you can see the paradox of IQ.

What I'll do in the remaining pages is explain how both facts can be true: how your personal IQ matters little for you as an individual, but how at the same time your nation's average IQ matters enormously for determining how much you earn, how much you produce, and how good your life feels. I'll also explain what policymakers and public health professionals may be able to do to raise a country's average IQ score. After all, if IQ is as important to a nation's prosperity as I claim, then raising a nation's average level of mental skills should be a top priority. Fortunately, here there are grounds for genuine hope: IQ isn't perfectly malleable—at least with the science of today—but neither is it etched in stone.

As you read the book, every so often you may start thinking, "But I know someone who does great on standardized tests who's done terribly in life, so how can IQ really matter that much for a country?" Remember: that puzzle is what this book is all about.

Do Your Nation's Test Scores Matter More Than Your Own?

Is there really evidence that nations with higher average scores on math and science tests are richer, more productive, faster growing? Do these test scores tell us more than if we just knew the average years of schooling in a country? That's what economists Eric Hanushek and Dennis Kimko wanted to find out.[3] For decades, international agencies have measured math, science, and reading skills in countries around the world. In recent years, the best-known of these testing programs have been PISA (Programme for International Student Assessment), TIMSS (Trends in Mathematics and Science Study), and PIRLS (Progress in International Reading Literacy Study). These are the widely publicized test scores that make the news every few years to let Americans know that their students are falling behind, and the test scores have been used by hundreds of scholars around the world. In 2000, Hanushek and Kimko published an influential study that drew on an earlier, related set of international math and science tests. Hanushek and Kimko's key finding has been replicated many times since then by scholars using a variety of international tests: test scores do a better job predicting an economy's performance than do years of education.

Perhaps that's no surprise. In many less developed countries, "years of schooling" don't include a lot of actual schooling. Economists and education researchers alike have found that in poor countries, students often don't have textbooks and teachers are often absent. That's not a recipe for learning. But there's more to the story than that. Another factor is that students in less developed countries *come to school* in a weaker position to learn. Children in these countries are more likely to have faced malnutrition and disease, both before and after they're born.

But Hanushek and Kimko did more than just find out that test scores are better predictors of national prosperity than years of education. They also found out that higher test scores have a much stronger relationship with *national* economic performance than with *individual* economic performance. Looking at how individual student test scores predicted those students' wages later in life, they found that individuals with higher test scores earned only slightly more than average within a given country, but nations with higher average test scores grew exceptionally fast. Here again is the paradox of IQ: standardized test scores—whether we call them IQ tests or math tests or something else—predict big national differences but only modest individual differences.

So yes, if you do better on math tests you'll probably earn more in life. But if an entire *nation* has higher average scores on math tests, it can probably look forward to a substantially more prosperous future. Nations with high test scores are usually either already rich or growing quite quickly, such as either France or China. The fact that average national test scores do a great job of predicting national economic performance has been found again and again in the economics and psychology literatures, but an *explanation* for why this is so has been harder to come by. Hanushek and Kimko themselves seem to think that the high test scores aren't really causing much extra growth: they say, "the [national] growth equation results are much larger than the corresponding results for individual earnings. . . ." and they also say, "the simple estimates of cross-country growth relationships appear to overstate the causal impact of" the test scores.[4]

But perhaps it's not an overstatement; perhaps it's a sign of a mental multiplier, a positive side effect of cognitive skills. Perhaps one person being good at standardized tests is just "interesting," but a whole nation of people who tend to be good at standardized tests is world-changing. In this book, I'll walk through some reasons rooted in mainstream economics, psychology, and political science to explain why the skills that standardized tests try to measure have bigger payoffs for nations than for individuals.

Test Scores Around the World

Let's start off by looking at the relationship between these test scores and income per person. Psychologist Heiner Rindermann and his coauthors have taken the widely used international PISA, TIMSS, and PIRLS test scores and converted them into a single national average "cognitive ability score" for each country.[5] Since national scores change over time, this is just a snapshot, but it will give us a sense of how test scores are distributed across countries. And of course, these averages hide a wide variation: there are high scorers in every nation.

Income per person differs massively across countries—by a factor of thirty to fifty between the few richest and the few poorest. So while pundits get worked up over the 30 percent differences in living standards between northern and southern Europe or between Japan and Taiwan, the real issue for human well-being is the 3,000 percent difference in living standards between the United Kingdom and some countries in sub-Saharan Africa. And just as it's challenging to measure cognitive abilities across countries, it's at least as challenging to measure national income across countries: neither are perfect measures. And keep in mind that the measurement problems for national income are worse in poorer countries, where government bureaucracies are more likely to be strongly politicized or where even well-intentioned officials just don't have the resources to make accurate measurements.[6]

Figure I.1, in which each dot represents a nation, shows that countries whose citizens tend to do well on these tests tend to earn more income per person in a year. The figure uses economists' favorite proxy for national income per person: gross domestic product (GDP) per person. GDP has the added benefit of focusing our attention on an economy's productivity, how many goods and services people actually produce in a year. As the figure shows, there are exceptions to the scores-predict-income rule in today's world, but most of the exceptions are modest. If you look at the high end of the scores, you'll notice that the average person in East Asia tends to do quite well on these tests, and you'll also see that most countries in East Asia (as well as high-scoring Singapore) have been economic success stories for the past half century.

Take a look at the lower-income countries in the graph, and

The Paradox of IQ   9

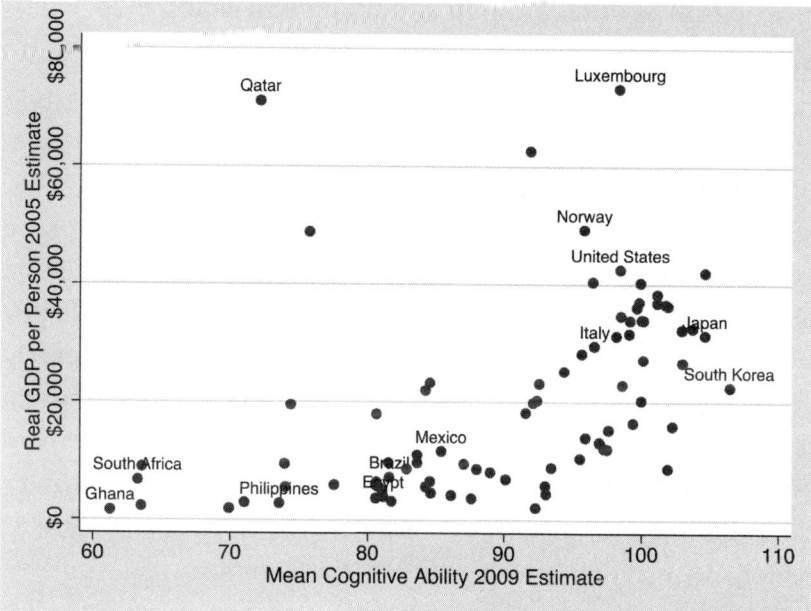

FIGURE I.1 Average cognitive ability estimated in 2009 from earlier PISA, TIMSS, and PIRLS international exams and estimated 2005 GDP per person
Sources: Rindermann, Sailer, and Thompson, "The Impact of Smart Fractions," and Penn World Tables 7.1.

you'll see a general rule along with some exceptions. The countries in the bottom half of the graph have low average test scores with a few exceptions: the poorer nations with scores in the low 90s tend to be former communist countries, perhaps still recovering from decades of economic mismanagement. And some of the wealthier countries with lower average scores tend to be rich in natural resources.

This brings us to the lower-left-hand corner, countries where poverty is all too common and where worker productivity is currently low. On average, people in these countries have done poorly on standardized tests. Of course, there are high-scoring people in every country, but on average people in the poorest countries tend to do poorly on standardized tests.

Test Scores: Shaped by School and Much Else

While I've spoken about math and science tests, from here on I'll mostly focus on IQ tests and other similar tests. IQ-type tests—sometimes called intelligence tests, though my fellow economists often wisely prefer the term *cognitive skill tests*—are good choices for a few reasons. For one, IQ tests have been given in many more countries around the world than have the PISA and TIMSS tests: elementary schools around the world have IQ test scores already sitting in filing cabinets. Second, many of these IQ tests are purely visual pattern-finding tests that don't obviously draw on school learning, so compared to a science test these IQ tests might be more fair and less biased; we'll return to the issue of test bias in Chapter 2. And third, once we start discussing IQ rather than generic "test scores," we can draw on a century of research by psychologists, infectious disease specialists, nutritionists, and others on ways to raise IQ scores and the skills these tests attempt to measure. IQ tests are the standard measure of cognitive skills across many disciplines, and it's good to stick with the standard. "Math score" gets most people thinking about good teachers, good books, good educational psychology—all important ways of improving cognitive skills. But we can't forget that people's skills are shaped well before they begin school and are shaped by forces outside of school. By talking about IQ, it will be hard to ignore life outside the classroom.

Test Scores and Prosperity: Just a Coincidence?

Should you put much weight on these results so far? After all, rich countries and poor countries differ in countless ways, and average test scores are just one of the differences. I could just as easily have shown a graph that shows that rich countries have more cell phones per person, or that people in rich countries eat at restaurants more often or are more likely to have vacation homes. Does Figure I.1 really tell us anything about what drives the wealth of nations?

One preliminary check is to see whether a nation's average test scores still do a good job of predicting a nation's level prosperity even when you know a lot of other things about the country: this approach is known as multiple regression. It amounts to asking, "Even if I already know that your country has a high savings rate, a lot of mineral wealth, or whatever, does knowing your nation's average test scores still help me to predict how productive your country is?" In a paper I coauthored with psychologist Joel Schneider, we used rough estimates of each nation's average IQ score to predict prosperity. We found that in hundreds of statistical tests, even if you knew which region of the world the country was in, even if you knew its religious background, even if you knew how open it was to global trade, it turned out that a nation's estimated average IQ was a good predictor of a nation's level of prosperity.[7] National test scores predict national productivity.

You might be wondering why some countries have higher average scores and others have lower average scores. That's an important question, but it's a question this book isn't designed to answer. This isn't a book about where a nation's IQ comes from, it's a book about where a nation's IQ takes it.

I have a good reason for focusing on where IQ can take a nation: it's an important overlooked topic. Also, there are already a lot of books and articles of varying quality about why IQ and other test scores differ from person to person and from country to country. I will discuss some of this research, partly because it is so fascinating and partly because I want to encourage more people to think about the topic. If higher average IQ is important to national economic outcomes, then it's important to find ways to raise these skill levels for each and every nation. If higher average IQ is important, it's time to start reading the high-quality books about raising national test scores and national cognitive skills.

There are good reasons to believe that national IQ scores can rise—and the best reason is because they already have. In the rich countries, IQ scores have consistently risen over the twentieth century, a phenomenon known as the Flynn Effect, after the philosopher—the *philosopher*, mind you—who discovered it. We'll talk about Flynn's world-shaking research in Chapter 3, but keep the Flynn Effect in mind when people tell you that IQ can't be changed.

Collective Intelligence: Each Nation as Hive Mind

Animal researchers, computer scientists, and occasionally social scientists sometimes use the metaphor of "collective intelligence" or a "hive mind" to explain group actions. Why do animal herds run together to avoid predators, dodging this way and that? How do honeybees and ants share information and collaborate to build vast structures and complex economies that no one insect could ever build alone? Indeed, human society in every nation today is a form of collective intelligence, in which the accumulated knowledge of the past makes its members richer today, and in which the many small, daily cognitive contributions of millions of their neighbors—in offices, in factories, in the halls of government, and elsewhere—help to make their lives better as if by Adam Smith's invisible hand. Those millions of small cognitive contributions are what create each nation's collective intelligence, each nation's hive mind. Members of society all draw on that collective intelligence, they all get benefits from the hive mind that they never pay for, benefits that, by my lights at least, they don't deserve. And it's typically better to be the less-skilled honeybee in the highly productive hive than to be the highly skilled honeybee in the less-productive hive: your neighbors have an important influence on what you can accomplish. That the hive mind exists for every nation is almost obvious. The key question is whether a nation's average IQ scores are an important driver of the hive mind.

It Pays to Be Around the Cognitively Skilled

In the next three chapters we'll review the basics of modern IQ research: brain scans and job performance and nutrition and whether we really can compare average test scores across countries. Then in Chapters 4 through 9, I'll lay out five major channels for how IQ can pay off more for nations than for you as an individual:

1. High-scoring people tend to save more, and some of that savings stays in their home country. More savings mean more machines, more computers, more technology to work with, which helps make *everyone* in the nation more productive.

2. High-scoring groups tend to be more cooperative. And cooperation is a key ingredient for building higher-quality governments and more productive businesses.

3. High-scoring groups are more likely to support market-oriented policies, a key to national prosperity. People who do well on standardized tests also tend to be better at remembering information, and informed voters are an important ingredient for good government.

4. High-scoring groups will tend to be more successful at using highly productive team-based technology. With these "weakest link" technologies, one misstep can destroy the product's value, so getting high-quality workers together is crucial. Think about computer chips, summer blockbuster films, corporate megamergers.

5. The human tendency to conform, at least a little, creates a fifth channel that multiplies the effect of the other four: the imitation channel, the peer effect channel. Even a small tendency to conform, to act just a little bit like those around us, to try to fit in, tends to quietly shape our behavior. If you have cooperative, patient, well-informed neighbors, that probably makes you a bit more cooperative, patient, and well-informed.

Of course, test scores don't explain *everything* about the wealth of nations: I'm only claiming that IQ-type scores explain about half of everything across countries—and much less within a country. If your next-door neighbor earns a lot more or less than you, it's not mostly because of IQ. And across countries, differences in geography, culture, and the long reach of colonialism are surely shaping the wealth of nations. The hive mind is no single-cause theory of prosperity. It's just a story that almost no one else is talking about.

Chapter 1

JUST A TEST SCORE?

HERE'S THE MOST IMPORTANT FACT ABOUT IQ TESTS: skill in one area predicts skill in another. If a person has an above-average score on one part of an IQ test—the vocabulary section, for instance—she probably has an above-average score on any other part of the test. A thorough IQ test such as the Wechsler or the Stanford-Binet actually contains about a dozen separate tests. So check to see whether that person did well on solving the vocabulary test: if she did, she's probably better than average at memorizing a long list of numbers, she could probably look at the drawing of a person talking to a police officer and instantly realize that the officer is standing knee-deep in water, and she probably did better than average on the wood block puzzle.

That's the real surprise of IQ tests and other cognitive tests: high scores in one area tend to go along with high scores in other areas, even ones that don't outwardly appear similar. Psychologists often talk about the "general factor of intelligence," the "g factor," or the "positive manifold," but let's call it "the da Vinci Effect," since Leonardo's excellence spanned so many subjects from painting to clock design to military engineering. The da Vinci Effect means that our parents and grandparents are usually wrong when they tell us "everything balances out in the end" or "if you're weak in one area that just means you're stronger in another." When it comes to IQ tests—*on average*—if a person is stronger in one area, that's a sign the person is probably stronger at other tasks as well.

We'll return to the notion of the da Vinci Effect a lot, so it's a concept worth understanding well. The claim isn't that *every* relationship between mental skills is *always* strongly positive—there are always exceptions to every rule, just as there are people who smoke two packs a day and live to be ninety. But, as we'll see in this chapter, many of the most commonly recognized general skills have strong positive relationships, and it's rare to find any sort of negative relationship across large groups of people.

IQ tests are often the stuff of controversy. What can they really tell us? What can they actually measure? What real-world outcomes can they help us to predict? That's exactly what we'll discuss in this chapter. It's going to focus *exclusively* on studies done in rich countries, studies in which test subjects are reasonably healthy and have some prospect of a real education. And I make a claim that, in these settings, the mainstream of psychology is also comfortable making: IQ tests are a rough, imperfect measure of what the typical person would call general intelligence.

Of course, a test score is just a test score until we've seen real evidence that it predicts something beyond other test scores. But when we see that the da Vinci Effect turns up repeatedly during IQ tests in today's rich countries, we know we're getting closer to the real-world version of intelligence: the ability to solve a variety of problems, quickly recall different types of information, and use deductive reasoning in multiple settings. When ordinary people say someone is intelligent, they usually mean that the person has mental skills that span a wide range. They mean that that person's mental skills have at least a touch of the da Vinci Effect.

"True on Average"

I discuss a lot of facts in this book and make a lot of claims about general tendencies. It should go without saying but bears repeating when discussing the important topic of human intelligence: these statements are only true on average. There are many exceptions; in fact almost every case is an exception, with about half of the cases turning out better than predicted and half turning out worse.

It would be tedious if I had to repeat the phrases "true on average" or "this relationship has many exceptions" or "tends to predict" every single time I make a factual claim. So I won't. But remember: every data-driven claim in this book is only a claim about the general tendency, and there are always exceptions. Every person we meet, every nation we visit, is an exception to the rules—but it's still a good idea to know the rules.

Intelligence: As with Strength or Size, Oversimplification Often Helps

Suppose you were given a hundred computers and told your job was to figure out which ones were faster than others. There's one catch: you don't know the actual processor speed of any of the computers. How would you rank them? You might try running ten or twenty different pieces of software on each of them—a video game or two, a spreadsheet, a word processor, a couple of web browsers. For each computer, you could write down, on a scale of 1 to 100, how fast the computer runs each piece of software, and then average those numbers together to create a computer speed index for each computer. Of course, the process won't be entirely fair—maybe you unintentionally chose a spreadsheet program that was designed specifically for one type of computer—but it's a step in the right direction. Further, it's probably better than just trying out one or two applications indiscriminately on each computer for half an hour and then writing up a subjective review of each machine. Structuring the evaluation process probably makes it fairer.

Now suppose you were trying to assess the overall physical strength of a hundred male Army recruits. You know that some people are great at carrying rocks and some are great at pushups and so on, but you also suspect that, on average, some people are just "stronger" than others. There will be tough cases to compare, but perhaps you could create a set of ten athletic events—call it a decathlon. People who do better in each event get more points. Wouldn't the people with the ten highest scores generally be quite a bit stronger—in the common sense of the word—than those with the ten lowest scores? Of course they would. There'd be an exception here and there, but the ranking would work pretty well. And here's a big claim you'll probably agree with: recruits who did the best in the decathlon would usually be better at other lifting-punching-carrying tasks that weren't even part of the decathlon. The decathlon score would help predict nondecathlon excellence.

Again, an index, an average, will hide some features that might be important. But for large, diverse populations, there is almost surely a da Vinci Effect for strength. It's not impossible for an adult male who benches only seventy-five pounds to be great at pull-ups, but it will be relatively rare. Usually, strength in one area will predict strength in others. Some people are on average "stronger" overall. You get the point: the da Vinci Effect comes up in areas of life other than discussions of mental skill. In these other, less sensitive areas, it's easy to see the value of a structured test. We get the same benefit by measuring intelligence in a structured way.[1]

It was psychologist Charles Spearman who began the century-long study of the da Vinci Effect. In a 1904 study of students at a village school in Berkshire, England, Spearman looked at student performance in six different areas: the classics (works written in Greek and Latin), as well as French, English, math, discrimination of musical pitch, and musical talent.[2] And while it's perhaps obvious that people who did better at French would usually be better at Greek and Latin, it's not at all obvious that people with better musical pitch would be substantially better at math—and yet that's what Spearman found.

But Spearman went further than that—he asked whether it was reasonable to sum up all of the data into just two categories: a "general factor" of intelligence, and a residual set of skills in each specific area. If you tried to sum up a person's various academic skills—or later, his test scores—with just one number, just one "general factor," how much information would you throw away? We do this kind of data reduction every time we sum up your body temperature with just one number. (You know you're not the same temperature everywhere, right?). We also do this when we sum up a national economy's productivity by its "gross domestic product per person" (which hides the various strengths and weaknesses of the medical sector, the restaurant sector, and so on), or even when we describe a person as simply "nice" or "mean." Whether the simplification works well is a practical matter—so how practical is it to sum up all of your cognitive skills on a variety of tests with just one number?

As it turns out, it actually works pretty well. Here's one way to sum it up for modern IQ tests: this "general factor," this "*g* factor," this weighted average of a large number of test scores, can summarize 40 to 50 percent of all of the differences across people on a modern IQ test.[3] Some people do better on math sections, some do better on verbal sections, some do better on visual puzzles—but almost half the overall differences across all tests can be summed up with one number. Not bad for an oversimplification.

At the same time, this *g* factor in mental skills helps to explain why reasonable, well-informed people can dispute the value of IQ tests. On the one hand, it's great to know that one number can sum up so much. On the other hand, a little more than half of the information is still left on the table—so if you're hiring someone just to solve math problems or just to write good prose, you'd obviously want to know more than just that one overall IQ score. What the *g* factor can tell you is that your math expert probably has a good vocabulary.

Measuring Cognitive Skills: A Rainbow of Diverse Methods

It's worth noting that the most comprehensive IQ tests aren't like normal tests; they're structured more like interviews. Some skeptics dismiss IQ tests as just measuring whether you're good at staring at a piece of paper, coming up with an answer, and writing it down. But the comprehensive IQ test used most often today—the Wechsler mentioned earlier—involves little paper-staring and almost no pencils. The person giving the test (a psychologist or other testing expert) asks you why the seasons change or asks you to recite a list of numbers that she reads out to you. You answer verbally. Later you are handed some wooden puzzle blocks and you try to assemble them into something meaningful.

And on one section, you do actually take a pencil to mark down your answers. Your job on this "coding test" is to translate small, made-up characters into numbers using the coding key at the bottom of the page. The circle with a dot inside stands for 4; an "X" with a parenthesis next to it stands for 7. Code as many as you can in a minute or two. (Note that I am not using actual items from IQ tests here. I just use examples that are similar. One doesn't give away answers to IQ test questions.)

However, some more rudimentary IQ tests really are just written multiple-choice exams, and one of them plays an important role throughout this book and in economic research: Raven's Progressive Matrices. Take a look at Wikipedia's sample Raven's question (Figure 1.1): What kind of shape in the lower-right corner would complete the pattern?[4] Fortunately, the real Raven's is mul-

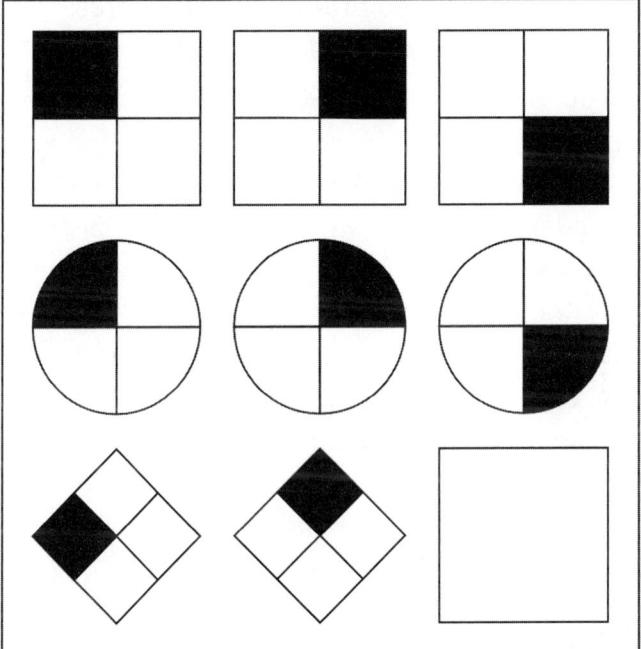

FIGURE 1.1 A problem similar to those on the Raven's Progressive Matrices
Source: http://en.wikipedia.org/wiki/File:Raven_Matrix.svg (Under Creative Commons License, from user Life_of_Riley)

tiple choice, so you needn't solve it yourself. In all these questions, the goal is to look for a visual pattern and then choose the option that completes the pattern.

The questions eventually get quite difficult. The lower-right corner is always blank, and you choose the best multiple-choice response. Raven's is popular because it can easily be given to a roomful of students at once (no need for one tester per student) and because it *appears* (note the italics) to have fewer cultural biases than some other IQ tests: the test doesn't measure your vocabulary, your exposure to American or British history, your skill at arithmetic, or any other obviously school-taught skill. Most people don't practice Raven's-style questions at school or at home, so training (which obviously can distort IQ scores artificially) might not be much of a concern.

Verbal Scores Predict Visual Scores Predict Verbal Scores

The *g* factor or da Vinci Effect means that your scores on one part of an IQ test predict your scores on other parts. But how well do they do that? Is it almost perfect? And if so, what does an "almost perfect" relationship look like in the real world? Here's one example: the relationship between the heights of identical twins. Identical twins are almost always almost exactly the same height as each other.[5]

Throughout this book, when two measures have a relationship that strong, I'll call that a "nearly perfect" or "almost perfect" relationship.[6] The two measures don't have to be recorded in the same units: the average monthly Fahrenheit temperature in Washington, D.C., has a nearly perfect relationship with the average monthly centigrade temperature in Baltimore, for instance, rising and falling together over the course of a year. Another example of a "nearly perfect" relationship is your IQ measured this week versus your IQ measured next week. A few people have exceptionally good or bad test days, but they're not common enough to weaken the nearly perfect relationship. Even more relevant: in one study, a person's adult IQ has an almost perfect relationship with his IQ five years later.[7]

A slightly weaker but still strong relationship exists between the body mass index (BMI) of identical twins raised apart.[8] BMI is a complicated ratio of weight and height that is used to measure whether people are over- or underweight. You can imagine why this relationship might be a bit weaker than the height relationship: some parents feed their kids more calories, some kids live in towns where sports are popular, and so on. But the rule that identical twins have similar BMI is still extremely useful. This is what we'll call a "strong" or "robust" relationship. This is like the relationship between your IQ when you're a teenager and your IQ when you're in middle age, at least in the rich countries. High scorers in tenth grade are almost always above-average scorers in middle age, with some doing noticeably better than before and some doing noticeably worse. Here, the exceptions are interesting, noticeable, an area for future research, but only a fool would ignore the rule.[9] For instance, the link between national average test scores and national income per person is strong.

Slightly weaker relationships need their own expression, and we'll call those "modest" or "moderate" relationships.[10] Here, big exceptions are extremely common, but if you're comparing averages of small groups of people, you'll still see the rule at work. An example we're all familiar with is the relationship between height and gender. Men are usually taller than women, but enormous exceptions abound: indeed, few would protest the statement "men are taller than women" because we all know it's just a generalization. These "modest" or "moderate" relationships sometimes exist between different parts of an IQ test or across very different kinds of IQ tests. For example, one study of third graders found a moderate relationship between a child's Raven's score and her vocabulary scores—but the same study found a strong, robust relationship between vocabulary scores and overall reading skills in the third grade, and by the fifth grade even the Raven's score had a robust relationship with reading skills.[11] As people get older, the relationships across different parts of an IQ test tend to grow more robust.

This is one of the surprising yet reliable findings of the past century: visual-spatial IQ scores have moderate to robust relationships with verbal IQ scores, so you can give one short test and have a rough estimate of how that person would do on other IQ tests. My fellow economists and I have taken advantage of this aspect of the da Vinci Effect in our research. We often have test subjects take the Raven's matrices since it has a moderate to robust relationship with other IQ test scores and it's quite easy to hand out copies of the written test to groups of students.

Anything less than a "modest" relationship I'll call a "weak" relationship. That's like the relationship between height and IQ.[12] The relationship is positive, but much taller people only have slightly higher than average IQs. The relationship isn't nothing, but it's an effect that will only be noticeable when you compare averages over large numbers of people. Typically, a group of women who are six feet tall are probably just a little bit smarter than a group of women who are five feet tall, with the emphasis on "just a little bit." You should still do the job interview even if she walks through the door at 4'11".

IQ Without a Test

Wouldn't it be wonderful if we could get a rough measure of someone's IQ, their average set of mental skills, without having to give any test at all? That way, all the arguments about test bias, language skills, and who went to a good school could fade into the background and we could have a useful, if only somewhat accurate, measure of a person's IQ. Fortunately, the past few decades have presented us with just such a measure, and it comes from an MRI machine. Yes, magnetic resonance imaging, the same device that's used to scan for tumors and heart disease.

IQ researchers use the MRI to definitively answer a question that people have asked for centuries: Do smarter people usually have bigger brains? The answer, on average, is a very clear "yes." The correlation between a person's IQ and his brain size is modest or moderate: big exceptions abound, but the rule is still there. There are so many studies looking at the IQ-to-brain-size question that there are now reviews that look at all the relevant studies and textbooks that review the reviews. Three quotes—two from textbooks published by Oxford and Cambridge University presses, and a third from a book in Oxford's excellent *Very Short Introduction* series, give us the story:

> Although the overall correlation between brain size and intelligence is not very high, there can be no doubt of its reliability.[13]

> Clearly overall brain size is correlated with intelligence test scores. The [modest] correlation... is not everything, but is not to be dismissed.[14]
>
> To the best that we can judge, then, the untutored guess that the cleverer person is literally more "brainy" has some modest force.[15]

The author of the second quote, psychologist Earl Hunt, goes on to say that even though science has verified the rough accuracy of the IQ-to-brain-size relationship,

> I doubt there will be any great effort to develop this finding any more....[16]

The reason he gives? The same MRI technology that verified the relationship has made it possible to search for the precise regions of the brain that are associated with individual cognitive skills, so one can stop looking at size and start looking for locations. The path to understanding the *how* of intelligence is likely to run through the *where* of individual mental processes. I won't pursue these fascinating questions further, but this new frontier illustrates how MRI technology is allowing researchers to search for the precise brain processes that form the structure of intelligence.

What does the modest relationship between brain size and IQ really tell us about the nature of intelligence? By itself, not much. Nobody thinks the weak link between IQ and height is evidence that height by itself makes a person smarter, so we should be similarly cautious about concluding that a bigger brain makes a person smarter. But the modestly reliable link between IQ and brain size is useful all the same. Critics of IQ testing often claim that the tests are biased in this way or that, and these claims deserve serious attention. However, it's unlikely that the IQ tests and the MRI machines both share the same bias. IQ researchers have found still other predictors of IQ, predictors that aren't at all like traditional IQ tests, predictors that get closer to the idea that the brain is a computer that processes information. These predictors remind us that while speed isn't everything, some computers are faster than others and faster is usually better.

Quick!

You're looking at a screen and an image flashes quickly in front of you for half a second. Hmm—was that the letter F or the letter L? You say "F" out loud and soon another image flashes—this time for a quarter-second. Again, you give your best guess, another F. Then an eighth of a second flash, a sixteenth, and so on. Shorter and shorter flashes of the image make it harder to guess correctly each time.

The images are usually simple shapes, like a regular C or a backwards one, and your job is to note, for instance, whether the C is open to the left or the right. Often you won't have to say the words "left" or "right"; you'll just toggle a switch to the left or right.

So at what point would you no longer be able to do better than random at correctly answering "left" or "right"? When the image flashes for just an eighth of a second? A 32nd? A 128th? That's the key variable the researcher keeps track of in this study. Some people are essentially guessing when it's anything less than a 16th of a second, some find that's more than enough time. Of course, there's one other variable the researcher wants to measure: your conventional IQ score. Studies that compare IQ to how much time you need to inspect the image are known, unsurprisingly, as "inspection time" studies.

Can it possibly be the case that people who only need to see the image for a tiny fraction of a second tend to have higher average IQ scores than people who need to see it for an eighth or sixteenth of a second? Summarizing "dozens of studies" run on "four continents" dating back to the 1970s, psychologist Ian Deary says,

> [t]he overall answer is yes, there is a moderate association between how good people are at the inspection time test and how well they score on intelligence tests.[17]

Another review of inspection time studies found that people with shorter inspection times—people who could more quickly identify the image—not only tended to have higher overall IQs, but in particular tended to be better at the more abstract parts of the IQ test. Good "inspectors" tended to be better at visual, Raven's-type puzzles, but perhaps not that much better at trivia and vocabulary questions.[18] Inspection time tests get us closer to the idea of IQ as processing speed, but at the same time these tests show that processing speed isn't the whole story of IQ—just as brain size isn't the whole story.

A third kind of non-test test has been run many more times than the MRI and inspection time tests. You have a small computer panel in front of you, with a large button in the middle of the panel and four smaller buttons above it. The smaller buttons have lights in them. Your job is to hold down the large button until one of the smaller ones lights up; then, you touch the small lighted button as fast as you can. People who press the lighted button faster tend to have higher IQ scores. These simple tasks—"elementary cognitive tasks," or ECTs as they are known in the literature—have provided further evidence that there's more to IQ than book learning.

Reaction time studies have tended to focus on three measures: how quickly you press the target button, how quickly you take your finger off the large button when you see the smaller one light up, and how variable a person's responses are. Do you reliably react after exactly two tenths of a second, or do you react faster some times than others? People with higher IQ scores tend to be more stable, while those with lower scores respond more erratically. Overall, the relationship between IQ and most measures of reaction time is weak, weaker than IQ's relationship with brain size or with inspection time. But the relationship has been found so often and in so many different testing situations—partly because it's such a cheap experiment to run—that it's now a bedrock fact of modern

IQ research: people with higher IQs tend to press the lighted button faster. They tend, on average, to be quicker.

Your Job Is a Test, Too

IQ tests help predict scores on other IQ tests, even tests that are quite unlike each other. And IQ tests help predict brain size and some kinds of mental and even physical quickness. But how well do IQ tests predict how effective you will be at work? Here, the answer is unequivocal and backed by decades of research: IQ tests do about as well as the best kinds of job interviews—*structured* job interviews, in which the interviewer carefully designs the questions beforehand and sticks to the same ones with each candidate—and IQ tests are better than most of the methods people use to choose employees. Most human resource management textbooks will tell you the same story, probably citing one of management professor Frank Schmidt and psychologist John Hunter's summary analyses of hundreds of IQ and job performance studies.

No method of hiring is perfect, or even close to perfect, at picking the best workers—for instance, the relationship between IQ scores and eventual worker performance is modest to strong at best. But IQ tests are as good as anything that exists in the real world. And here's one useful finding: you're much better off forming your opinion of a worker based on her IQ score than basing it on a check of her references or (worst of all) a handwriting analysis.[19]

In addition, it appears that IQ tests are even better at predicting outcomes when the job requires higher skills. Back in the 1960s, the Bell Telephone System gave its entry-level management trainees an IQ-type test along with a number of personality tests. Bell's human resources division kept the test results a secret for two decades, even from other employees in the firm. When, after two decades, the company looked back to see which tests did the best job of predicting which trainees eventually rose the highest in the company hierarchy, the IQ-type test did the best job, beating out the personality tests.[20] Looking across many studies of IQ in the elite workforce, one review says,

> [G]eneral cognitive ability is the best single predictor of executive/professional-level performance, just as it is of performance in the middle to high-end range of the general workforce.[21]

But IQ has predictive power among workers outside the elite. The U.S. military uses IQ tests routinely to screen recruits, and every year the military turns down potential recruits who do poorly on the tests. If IQ tests were useless in the workplace, the military would be foolish to turn down able-bodied, low-scoring men and women who were willing to serve. The U.S. military acts like it believes in the power of the da Vinci Effect.

And the military has sound evidence for taking IQ tests seriously. Research using the U.S. Army's vast datasets on soldier IQ and subsequent performance found that an enlistee's IQ score has a strong positive relationship with that soldier's "technical proficiency" and "general soldiering" skills. The researchers ran a comparison as well, testing one predictor of job success against another. They asked which better predicted a soldier's overall technical proficiency and general soldiering skills, IQ or a measure of their personality and temperament? IQ won the race quite handily: it had a strong relationship with these measures of job success, while personality was just a modest predictor of success. That said, the personality and temperament measure won in the attempt to predict a soldier's leadership skills, discipline level, and physical fitness—so again, IQ isn't everything, but it's not something you'd leave on the table.[22]

In most of these studies that look at the relationship between IQ and worker quality, the quality measure is subjective: you ask the worker's boss how well the worker did, and compare that judgment against the worker's IQ score. Some studies can look at somewhat more objective measures, such as sales per year for a salesperson, or successful sorties for a military pilot. The more objective the measure, the stronger the relationship usually is between IQ and the measure of worker quality. But there's another indirect measure of worker quality that's particularly popular among economists: wages. The United Way aside, most employers aren't running charities, so they only pay one worker more than another when they need to. And one reason they might have to pay a worker more is if he's especially productive or especially good at his job. After all, good workers are likely to get hired away if they aren't paid enough.

This is one reason why educated workers earn more than less educated ones: the educated workers can usually just *do more stuff better*. If that weren't the case and employers were usually wrong about the (moderate) link between education and worker productivity, then any upstart firm could just hire inexpensive, less educated workers, do just as good a job at making cars or pizzas or software, and pocket the massive profits. The low-education firms would have explosive growth, blowing away the competition that remained foolishly wedded to the idea that you had to pay more to get more. Pretty soon, it would be all the buzz in the management consulting world: *triple your profits by hiring the less educated!*

Of course, we don't see that, not as a general trend. At least in the private sector, there's usually a reason why one group of workers in a particular line of work gets paid more than another, and it's not because the owner of the firm is especially charitable or especially foolish: it's because the higher-paid group is accomplishing more. That said, things are more complicated across lines of work: you usually have to pay people more to take on risky jobs, and you don't have to pay them as much to do fun jobs. There will always be qualified people willing to play bass guitar in front of an audience for very little cash.

But as a rule, if we routinely see firms paying a lot for a set of skills, it's probably because that set of skills is genuinely productive.

How much more a group of workers is being paid will tell us how much the market values that set of skills. Well, how much does the market value IQ?

The Market Test: IQ and Wages

In 1957, a government agency in Wisconsin gave IQ tests to about three thousand teenage males, all high school graduates, and then checked up on the men later on in their lives, first at the age of thirty-five and again at the age of fifty-three.[23] As part of their study they asked some basic lifestyle questions, a bit about the subjects' education and their parent's education; they also used tax records to find out how much the teenagers' parents and later they themselves earned. It turns out that the subjects' teenage IQ scores did a better job of predicting their wages as they grew older! So it looks like your IQ is something that, at least in a rich country such as the United States, you "grow into." It takes a while for people to find their place in life, and that's true for finding a place to use your intelligence.

So when these men were fifty-three, how much did IQ pay? The payoff to a high IQ appears moderate. Those with IQs in the top 10 percent earned about 60 percent more than those in the bottom 10 percent.

Has the Payoff to IQ Risen?

Other researchers have looked at other samples of workers, some in rich countries such as the United States, some in poor countries, and they tend to come to roughly similar results. What's the overall picture of the IQ-wage relationship? Two of the great progressive economists of our time, Samuel Bowles and Herbert Gintis, coauthored a paper back in 2001 with the influential economist Melissa Osborne that looked at dozens of studies documenting the link between IQ and wages. Some social scientists had claimed that, in our postindustrial age, the labor market was placing more value on high-IQ workers; Bowles, Gintis, and Osborne wanted to see if that was the case.[24] They showed pretty conclusively that it wasn't. The market had valued IQ for decades, and it seemed to value IQ about as much in the early 1990s as it had in the early 1960s. Overall the IQ premium hadn't changed.

A recent study confirms this finding: it looks at how well a young person's IQ has predicted his or her level of education, occupational status, and income all the way from 1929 to 2003. The study, by sociologist Tarmo Strenze, assembled previous studies run in Europe, the United States, Canada, Australia, and New Zealand across the twentieth century and found that IQ overall had a moderate relationship with education and job status and a weak but positive relationship with income across the decades.[25] And most important for our purposes, the link between IQ and income neither weakened nor strengthened across the decades. Young people in the 1930s and young people in the 1990s alike tended to have a weak, positive relationship between their measured IQ and their later income. So the rumors of IQ's exploding importance have turned out to be wrong so far: it's a reasonable guess that they'll be wrong in the future as well. The paradox of IQ is likely to be with us well into the twenty-first century.

Coda: Intelligence Is a Key Ingredient in Emotional Intelligence

But isn't there more than just one kind of intelligence? Aren't emotional intelligence and social intelligence just as important as narrow IQ-type intelligence? The ability to read people, the ability to get along well with others—those skills are important, and IQ tests can't be measuring those skills, can they? Social skills seem so different from the abstract pattern-finding of some IQ tests—but then again, being able to remember relevant facts about people you met a few weeks ago or the ability to interpret an ambiguous social situation might involve some of the same memory and puzzle-solving skills that IQ tests try to measure. Does the da Vinci Effect show up in social settings too?

One might contend that it's even harder to measure social or emotional intelligence than it is to measure more conventional intelligence. But psychologists have tried: they've checked to see whether people with more social or emotional intelligence tend to have higher IQs, and so far it looks like they do. The relationship often isn't as strong as the relationship between, say, a person's vocabulary test scores and her score on the Raven's matrices, so there are many exceptions, but the results are clear: IQ scores predict practical social skills.

The link between social or emotional intelligence and IQ has been tested for decades. Back in the 1920s, one early social intelligence test, the George Washington Social Intelligence Test, actually found a moderate relationship with overall IQ. That social intelligence test asked about "judgment in social situations, memory for names and faces, and recognition of the mental states behind words."[26] Another social intelligence test had people look at "film clips of brief scenes" showing people's "emotional states, and their task was to identify that state." Such tests have a weak to moderate relationship with a person's IQ.[27]

Tests of emotional intelligence are better developed, and indeed there's now a widely used test for "EQ," the MSCEIT, the Mayer-Salovey-Caruso Emotional Intelligence Test. The MSCEIT measures both the perception side of emotional intelligence ("What is that person probably feeling?") and the reasoning side ("What is the best way to handle this awkward situation?"). And perhaps by now it will come as no surprise that people who do better on the MSCEIT tend to do better on the Raven's, an entirely visual-spatial IQ test. The relationship is modest but real: the da Vinci Effect is strong enough to span human relationships. But on its own, does EQ matter more than IQ? Let me turn it over to psychologist N. J. Mackintosh:

> Contrary to some popular claims . . . there is no convincing evidence that tests of social or emotional intelligence are a better predictor of success than IQ.[28]

Indeed, if you know a person's conventional IQ and you're trying to predict job or school performance, there's usually little benefit to learning that person's EQ scores. But the reverse isn't true: if all you know is a person's score on the MSCEIT or a similar test, there's real benefit to learning his IQ score. Intelligence tests predict emotional intelligence, and the two go together to some degree. But of the two, it's clear which is usually more valuable. Better average social skills are typically just another benefit of having a higher IQ score, and since the economy is a social system, those social skills may prove important in explaining why higher-scoring nations tend to be more productive.

Chapter 2

A DA VINCI EFFECT FOR NATIONS

MOST OF US WOULD WILLINGLY PLACE A $20 BET that the average classroom in East Asia will outperform the average classroom in South America on the vast majority of math tests. Maybe that will change in the next few decades—due to shifts in education, public health, or other factors. As of today, however, it's a pretty safe bet.

But can the same cognitive test, given in different countries, actually predict something more substantial, such as intelligence, mental alertness, or quickness? Posing an even larger question, do these allegedly narrow measures of test-taking ability predict real-world economic outcomes in different countries? In other words, can an IQ test, designed by American academics, help to predict which villagers earn more in rural Pakistan? Can IQ tests be fair in the diverse world we inhabit?

Let's consider how a fair IQ test might show that one nation currently has a higher average IQ score than another. Nation X might have better childhood nutrition than Nation Y, which causes Nation X to have taller, healthier children. And since the brain is a part of the human body, healthier children will tend to have better-functioning brains. If you had fair IQ tests—perhaps the Raven's pattern-finding test, which isn't language-bound—and administered it to typical children in both countries, you'd find that Nation X's students usually did better. The same traits that make the students in Nation X taller on average also make them smarter on average. And we'd expect that as Nation X's students grew up, they'd become more productive, higher-paid workers, able to think a bit more quickly on the job.

Now let's consider another scenario, the case of Nations P and Q. In Nation P, the students are given a test in their own language, by a psychologist who speaks it. In Nation Q, the students are given an IQ test in a language they only use about half the time—perhaps just at school—by a psychologist who barely speaks any of the country's languages; he's a graduate student who just flew in to give the tests and then he'll fly home. It would be no surprise if the students in Nation P did better on average than the students in Q: students in Q would barely understand the graduate student's instructions, and the test's translation would be awful. Even the best students would be grasping at straws to try to understand what the test was all about.

The P and Q example is an obvious case of test bias.[1] But it's not the difference in test scores that makes the test unfair for students in Nation Q: what makes the test unfair is that it wouldn't work. In Nation Q there would be a weaker relationship between test scores and student performance in real-world settings. The Q test scores would contain far more noise than the P test scores. Yes, the brightest students in the Q sample would be a bit more likely to figure out the meanings of the poorly translated test, but IQ tests are not foreign language tests. The results of a test given by a poorly trained graduate student who doesn't understand the local culture would be about as valuable as a medical exam written by someone who took half a semester of human anatomy.

But language and competent test administration aren't the only possible problems. There are surely cultural barriers to testing average cognitive skills across countries. If we're comparing test scores across countries, we want to be sure that the tests aren't systematically harder in Nation Q than in Nation P. Some questions on an IQ test just won't be good questions in certain cultures. For instance, one part of the Wechsler IQ test is a picture completion test, in which you look at a picture and decide what is missing. Examples from old, outdated tests include "Two people playing tennis on a court lacking a net, or a man in a bowling alley but with no ball in his hand . . ."[2] Those aren't reasonable test questions for people who've never seen a tennis court or a bowling alley. Of course, these are obvious examples, and these basic objections have been known to decades of psychologists: hence the long-standing psychological research project of creating tests that were "culture fair" or "culture reduced."

So we can't just assume that differences in average test scores are the same as differences in average mental skills. People might have genuinely useful skills, skills that are useful in the marketplace and in government, but skills that can't show up on unfair tests. At the same time, differences in test scores across countries might well reflect differences in skills that modern markets and modern governments genuinely value. After all, if we're interested in predicting success in the modern economy, at predicting the ability to analyze and use information as it exists from Japan to Italy to the United Kingdom, we'd want a test that picks up differences in the broad mental skills actually useful in these societies.

Perhaps people are all equally skilled in some unmeasurable way that doesn't show up on any standardized test and that doesn't show up in modern life outcomes. If so, perhaps future research can measure that form of deep equality. But we're interested in finding something more down to earth: standardized tests—math tests, reading tests, IQ tests—that can detect any differences that might exist across countries in the current average level of practical mental skills. It appears that tests like this actually exist.

IQ Scores Across Countries: Where Do They Come From?

For decades, psychologists, economists, and public health researchers have been administering IQ tests around the world and reporting the results in academic journals. But there was no systematic effort to collect and compare these scores across countries until psychologist Richard Lynn and political scientist Tatu Vanhanen took on the task in their 2002 book *IQ and the Wealth of Nations*.[3] Since then, Lynn has worked with coauthors to revise, correct, and extend that database; he has been the leading, but not the only, researcher to collect IQ scores across countries.[4] I'll refer to these databases, with due respect to his coauthors, as Lynn's.

Over the decades, Lynn has made inflammatory statements about average group differences in IQ, but his research is widely cited and given weight in mainstream psychology journals, even by his severest critics. Indeed, one widely discussed study used Lynn's data to argue that infectious disease holds down average IQs in some countries.[5] That study, with its call to raise IQ by fighting disease, was discussed in both *The Economist* and in the Bill and Melinda Gates Foundation's 2011 annual report; both *The Economist* and the Gates report showed graphs with Lynn's "National Average IQ" on the vertical axis and rates of disease on the horizontal axis.[6] Bill Gates himself noted, "Although an IQ test is not a perfect measure, the dramatic effect you see [between national IQ and national disease burdens] is a huge injustice." Gates's cautious use of Lynn's available data offers a good example for researchers: data can be far from perfect and still bring us closer to the truth.

Lynn's datasets have IQ estimates from over a hundred countries, based on more than one test for the majority of countries. The papers drew mostly from previously published academic studies—sometimes a study of a single typical elementary school classroom, sometimes a comparison of healthy and unhealthy children in the same town, sometimes a study of hundreds or thousands of students or adults. Lynn and his coauthors scoured the literature for relevant studies. The Raven's visual IQ test was the most common test measure, so cultural references and language issues were less of a concern than they might be otherwise: it puts us closer to Countries X and Y and less like the unfair tests in Countries P and Q. There were usually many IQ estimates for rich or heavily English-speaking countries, while poorer ones were more likely to rely upon one or two studies. Overall, in a country that had multiple IQ test scores the results tended to be similar: the many tests in the United States averaged around 98, the United Kingdom scores averaged slightly higher at 100, Japanese scores tended to be around 105, and so on. Some countries are only represented with noisy, low-quality IQ data, and of course that's a problem for economic data as well; particularly in the poorest nations economic statistics are often quite inaccurate. But with national average IQ as with national average income per person, multiple perspectives and multiple sources of data can give researchers a useful if incomplete picture of a nation. On this topic, I should also note an important book that does what Lynn did but for a smaller set of countries: *Culture and Children's Intelligence.*[7] The authors compare the same IQ test—the Wechsler—across about a dozen relatively rich countries. They indeed find that these countries differ slightly in their average IQs and find that more prosperous and better-educated countries tend to have higher scores.

While Lynn's datasets draw upon academic studies—mostly run by other researchers—those aren't his only sources. He also uses IQ samples assembled by psychological testing firms: when one of these companies wants to sell its IQ tests in a new country, it's valuable to have a large sample of test subjects in that country to help "standardize" the test, so school psychologists, prison psychologists, and other mental health professionals can accurately report, "This person is in the 30th percentile / 70th percentile / 99th percentile in our country." These standardization samples are often large, perhaps with a thousand test subjects, enough to raise our confidence that a high or low average test score isn't just a coincidence because the testing expert happened to walk into a particularly strong or particularly weak school that day. The standardization samples tend to yield average scores close to the other scores for the same country, offering some confidence that the smaller studies are generally a good place to start. But of course, the best way to see whether Lynn's data are reasonably accurate is to compare them against other datasets assembled by researchers—something that's been done repeatedly in the past decade. We'll turn to those comparisons later.

One strength of the Lynn databases is that they draw heavily on nonverbal tests, especially the Raven's. As my own research with Schneider has shown, even if we only use the Raven's test scores to predict a nation's economic productivity, even if we throw out all the rest of the data, the relationship between current national average Raven's IQ and national productivity is quite strong.[8] To round out his data, Lynn also draws on some math tests run by international agencies; this is reasonable because, while any one cognitive test might be an imperfect measure of a nation's current average IQ, combining multiple imperfect measures is more likely to give us a good estimate of average cognitive skill. Get five first-year nursing students to take a person's blood pressure, and average the score. That average might not be as good as one measure from an experienced nurse. But what you'll have is far better than no measure at all.

When Lynn and Vanhanen first published their landmark book, much of the media attention focused on minor differences in estimated IQ across Europe: Was Sweden with an estimated average IQ of 101 really smarter than Norway, which tied the United States with an estimated 98? These discussions of quibbles, of two or three IQ points, apparently exasperated Lynn and Vanhanen. Since British IQ is defined with an average of 100—Lynn treats British IQ as the Greenwich Mean Time of global IQ comparisons—and since the IQ range of 85 to 115 points spans roughly two-thirds of the British population, a two- or three-point difference is minor. In their next book they chided readers who obsessed over differences that were more likely a result of measurement error than of real differences in average cognitive skill. IQ scores are, at best, a rough measure of the average mental skills you're really interested in, just as your semester grade in a course is a rough measure of how well you understand the subject or just as your nation's reported economic growth statistics are a rough measure of how the economy has been doing. It's the big differences that we should focus on, and that's what we'll focus on here. I'll start by discussing the region of the world where average IQ scores are currently lowest: Africa south of the Sahara.

Current Average IQ in Sub-Saharan Africa: A Debate Between Psychologists

Let's begin with a quotation:

> There can be little doubt that Africans average lower IQs than do westerners.[9]

That quote isn't from Richard Lynn: it's from a paper coauthored by psychologist Jelte Wicherts, one of Lynn's leading academic critics. While Wicherts and coauthors noted that test bias might help explain the low scores in sub-Saharan Africa, they also said that health and nutrition improvements, better educational TV shows, and more interactive toys could be part of the path to raising average IQ scores in sub-Saharan Africa.

In a widely discussed set of papers, Wicherts and coauthors set out to systematically critique Lynn's various estimates of national average IQ in sub-Saharan Africa.[10] Indeed, Wicherts and coauthors (henceforth I'll just refer to Wicherts) did find evidence that Lynn tended to drop or exclude IQ scores from sub-Saharan Africa that were on the high side, studies that Lynn and coauthors often thought were based on elite, unrepresentative test subjects.[11] Further,

Lynn was likely to include low scores that Wicherts thought were of doubtful quality. Some of the studies in the Lynn database included schoolchildren who were malnourished or ill, sadly a common enough occurrence in this region of the world. One study used by Lynn noted that some children had so little schooling experience they did not know how to use a pencil correctly; a test score from such a child would be as invalid as my IQ score if I took the test in Japanese or Spanish. Lynn and Wicherts went back and forth in a series of articles, critiquing each other's arguments and choices, and the exchange is valuable for illustrating just how many judgment calls any researcher (or any national government) has to make when assembling a large dataset.

Lynn's 2002 estimate of current national average IQ in sub-Saharan Africa was 67, well outside the 85 to 115 range that covers two-thirds of the U.K. population. After responding to Wicherts's critiques and modifying his list of studies, Lynn raised that estimate to 70. That average is far below Lynn's average for East Asia (106) and well below the average of 100 in the United Kingdom. How big is the average IQ gap between the United Kingdom and the typical country in sub-Saharan Africa, according to Lynn? If you were looking at people within the U.K. population (where the average British citizen is at the 50th percentile) then a score of 70 is at about the 2nd percentile. One can see why Lynn's claims about average IQ in sub-Saharan Africa provoked such strong revulsion. Surely no nation can have an average set of cognitive skills that low. Can it? And the thought that an entire geographic region could have an average that low seems preposterous on its face.

But what did the apparently more cautious, more careful Wicherts report? He said that the average IQ in sub-Saharan Africa was about 82—corresponding to the 12th percentile in the United Kingdom. That's an improvement from 70, and it's an improvement that arose partly because Wicherts chose to throw out samples of students who came from families with nutrition problems and low socioeconomic status. The Wicherts average of 82 only includes samples of apparently healthy students from families that have typical socioeconomic status. And in a region of the world with as much poverty and disease as sub-Saharan Africa, that decision is quite likely to leave out substantial portions of the population.

To further test the data and get the best average, Wicherts wrote a separate paper that looked at only the best test samples—cases with large random samples of a sub-Saharan African nation's population that weren't skewed toward or away from highly educated test subjects and in which the test subjects weren't particularly ill or particularly healthy. When Wicherts threw out every even slightly questionable study, reducing his dataset from dozens of studies to less than ten, what did he find? Did he find clear signs that biased tests and biased data collection were at the heart of the Lynn estimates? Alas, no: Wicherts's best samples of students have an average (median) IQ score of 76. That's at the 5th percentile within the United Kingdom.

As a result of the debates between Lynn and Wicherts, we have better cognitive skill estimates that point to a couple of conclusions. First, researchers like myself who long to raise average cognitive skills in the poorest regions of the world up to the levels of East Asia have their work cut out for them. Second, people like myself making comparisons across countries should take account of the possibility that the lowest scores might be inaccurately low. In my own research I've typically performed analyses that either "round up" the lowest scores to the Wicherts level or made other statistical adjustments so that the lowest-scoring countries can't drive the overall results.

And finally, if IQ tests in sub-Saharan Africa are (imperfectly) measuring the same skills that employers seem to value in the rich countries, we would expect current sub-Saharan African workers to be less productive (on average) than workers in the rich countries. The first point is one for public health researchers to take note of;

the final point spurs us to look at the link between IQ and wages beyond the rich countries.

What Else Do the Scores Predict?

On this final point there's already a large academic literature. IQ tests given in poor countries—both in sub-Saharan Africa and elsewhere—predict something quite practical: real-world earning power. Multiple studies run in poor countries find that higher test scores predict higher wages.

Even in rural Pakistan, higher Raven's IQ predicts higher wages. One might think that thousands of miles away from the Western universities where the tests were designed, abstract IQ tests would have no power to predict which workers earned more and which earned less—but an IQ test made up of boxes and lines and circles had a modest ability to predict a person's wages across rural Pakistan, just like in the United States.[12] And if you ask why the scores can predict wages, you'll find your way back to the da Vinci Effect: the tendency of people with greater mental skills in one area to be above average in other areas means that people with high Raven's scores will tend to have better than average memories, better than average arithmetic skills, and better than average verbal comprehension skills. These tendencies, even if they are moderate, mean that high scorers are usually more valuable on the job and are usually able to get into more lucrative lines of work.

The Highest Average IQ Scores in the World: East Asia

In the 1920s and 1930s, psychologists working in Hawaii found that residents of Japanese or Chinese descent tended to have average or perhaps above average IQ; other researchers working around the same time in British Columbia came to similar conclusions.[13] Later researchers found that the high scores showed up particularly in visual-spatial tests, with scores on the verbal parts of the IQ tests turning up equal to or slightly lower than average. Since then, the finding has become routine: in populations of East Asian ancestry, whether in China, Japan, South Korea, Taiwan, Hong Kong, or Singapore—or among populations in the United States or Europe whose ancestors came from East Asia—visual-spatial IQ scores tend to be higher on average than those of Western Europeans and their descendants.

Country-level results go back decades. As early as the 1960s, studies in Taiwan and Hong Kong found average IQ scores slightly above the European average. This happened at a time when these countries' economies were growing fast, but were still poor by U.S. and U.K. standards. Any simple story that "wealth causes IQ" has to account for the puzzlingly high average scores found in Taiwan and Hong Kong decades ago, as well as the high scores found in the poverty-stricken but fast-growing China we all know about today. A healthy environment helps to boost IQ, but it can't be the whole story. The high average IQs of East Asia and Singapore have yet to be fully explained.

But if full explanation isn't yet possible, let's at least take a moment to survey national average test scores in this economically vibrant region. Earl Hunt notes that in the TIMSS math assessment, four of the top five highest-scoring countries are in East Asia, while the fifth is Singapore (although it should be noted that the People's Republic of China only tested students from prosperous Shanghai), and in the PISA math tests three of the five highest-scoring countries were in East Asia. On PISA reading scores, South Korea was in the global top five, while Japan and Hong Kong were both in the top fifteen. And comparing the average performance of ethnic groups in the United States, Hunt notes, "IQ scores and educational data present a consistent ordering . . . with (northeast) Asians slightly ahead of Whites . . ."[14] So both within the United States and around the world, the average cognitive skills of East Asians tend to be quite exceptional. Let's hope researchers can find practical ways to make those kinds of scores a possibility for every country.

da Vinci Across the Globe?

Does the da Vinci Effect hold up across countries? Do nations with high average math scores also have high average verbal scores and high average IQ scores? Or instead does it all balance out so that strength on one international test usually means weakness in another? Heiner Rindermann ran a variety of statistical tests and the answer was clear: high test scores predict high test scores, and there is a nearly perfect relationship between Lynn's rough national average IQ estimates and the PISA and TIMSS national average math, science, and reading scores.[15] Rindermann and co-authors later combined these scores with the PIRLS literacy test to create a national estimate of what they call "cognitive ability." Figure 2.1 shows that when combined into a single index, the PISA, TIMSS, and PIRLS scores have a nearly perfect relationship with Lynn's National Average IQ estimate; these cognitive ability and IQ estimates are also reported in the Data Appendix. It's worth remembering that even this "nearly perfect" overall relationship still means exceptions for individual countries, particularly among the lower-scoring nations where accurate skill measurement is difficult. The slightly weaker relationship between the separately administered PISA and TIMSS is still robust, as it is between the PISA and the PIRLS, and the same strong relationship holds when one compares a handful of other cross-country cognitive tests. Rindermann finds strong evidence for a da Vinci Effect, a *g* factor, across countries. A country that displays high cognitive skills in one measured area probably has strong cognitive skills in other measured areas. I'll draw on this fact repeatedly: for nations, a high average score on one standardized test predicts high scores on others.

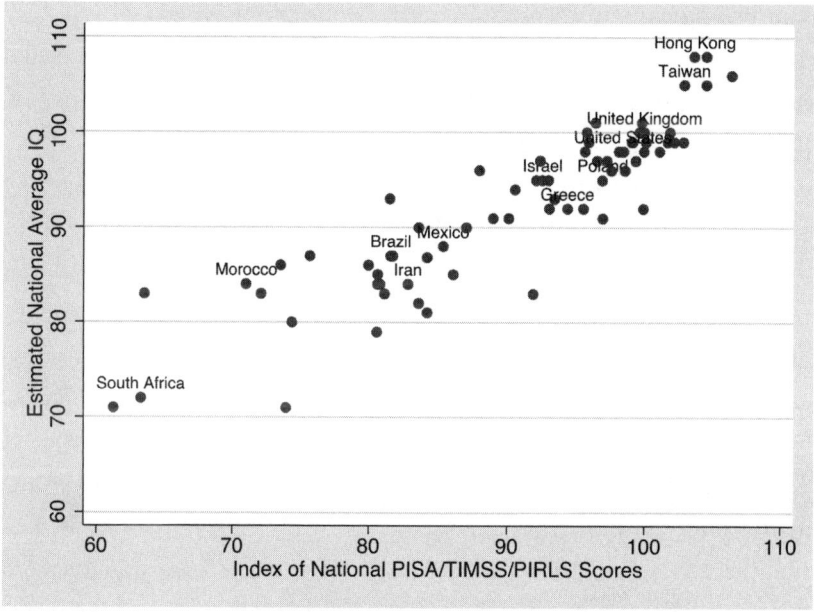

FIGURE 2.1 National average cognitive ability estimated from PISA, TIMSS, and PIRLS exams compared with national average IQ estimates

Sources: Rindermann, Sailer, and Thompson, "The Impact of Smart Fractions" and Lynn and Meisenberg, "National IQs calculated."

Measuring "Unmeasured" Differences in Immigrant Skill

Economists have long wondered why some immigrants to the United States succeed while others fail. Can national average IQ help to explain why? Do immigrants from lower-scoring countries earn less than those from higher-scoring countries? In a project with psychologist Joel Schneider, I addressed these questions. Using economist Lutz Hendricks's estimate of how much immigrants from different countries earn on average after coming to the United States, Schneider and I checked to see if those from higher-scoring countries earned more than those from lower-scoring countries.[16] The answer was an emphatic "Yes, but." Yes there was a positive relationship, but the relationship was modest: in fact, we found that immigrants from higher-scoring countries earned only slightly more than those from lower-scoring countries. And it looked like the relationship was about the same as in the Wisconsin study of IQ and earnings: one IQ point predicted about 1 percent higher earnings. An average immigrant from a country with an average IQ of 100 (the U.K. average) would earn about 10 percent more than the average immigrant from a country with an average score of 90.

We were also able to see if the result was just because immigrants from different countries tended to arrive with different education levels—Western European immigrants to the United States tend to have more officially measured education, for instance.[17] That wasn't the story: even when we only used the education-adjusted data, so that the only source of wage differences was what Hendricks had called "unmeasured worker skill," national average IQ still predicted about the same one point for 1 percent earnings difference. National IQ measured some of the unmeasured. So immigrants who arrive from countries with lower average cognitive skills don't really earn that much less on average, and immigrants from high-skill countries don't typically earn that much more. At the same time, my project with Schneider showed that the Lynn IQ estimates can predict yet another test score: they can predict how well immigrants do on the market test.

Chapter 3

JAMES FLYNN AND THE QUEST TO RAISE GLOBAL IQ

ECONOMIST STELLA QUIMBO WANTED TO FIND OUT how to raise IQ scores for children in the Philippines.[1] With a team of medical and economic researchers, she and her colleagues tested hundreds of Filipino children, giving them IQ tests and blood tests and interviewing the children's parents to learn a little about the backgrounds of the children. What they learned has been learned many times over in poor countries: unhealthy environments predict low average IQ. Children should have essentially zero lead in their blood, but the average child in Quimbo's sample had 7 micrograms of lead per deciliter. In their study, every extra microgram of lead predicted a three-point fall in IQ scores.

But of course just because lead exposure *predicts* low average IQ, that doesn't mean we can conclude that lead exposure *causes* low average IQ. Low-scoring kids might tend to come from low-scoring families for a variety of reasons: the apple usually doesn't fall far from the tree, as dozens of IQ studies have documented. For instance, low-scoring families tend to earn less money and therefore can't easily afford to live in nice, clean neighborhoods. So low test scores might cause the lead exposure rather than the other way around. Or some third force such as social oppression could cause both low IQ and the lead exposure.

How easy is it to raise average IQ for a nation? Is it merely a matter of giving kids healthy environments, good nutrition, and some decent schooling? Are East Asia–style average IQ scores just a few simple policy changes away for every nation on earth? I don't have an answer to that question—I don't know that anyone does as of this writing—but here's one piece of evidence that it's possible for average IQ scores to increase for an entire nation: it has already happened time and again in the twentieth century. In the rich countries, it appears that average IQ scores rose in every country for which data exist at a rate of perhaps two or three points per decade, an astonishing rate of increase.

The rise in national IQ was first documented in the United States: the U.S. Army gave IQ tests to World War I inductees, and, as the U.S. military does, it saved the data and the test forms. After World War II erupted and the Army began giving the old test to a new generation of draftees, Professor Read Tuddenham compared the average scores across the two groups of draftees.[2] The result was striking: the draftees of World War II had test scores averaging about fifteen points higher than draftees of World War I, triple the current IQ gap between, for example, the United Kingdom and Taiwan. Because there were so many test takers, there was no chance it was a fluke. Somehow, on a relatively abstract IQ test given around 1940, Americans from across the fruited plain seemed smarter than their fathers who had fought in the Great War. Later, in the early 1980s, Richard Lynn began looking at the IQ scores he and others had collected in Japan over the course of a half-century and noticed a similar pattern: average scores rising over time. But as with the Army findings, the Lynn finding of rising national IQ had no real impact on psychology: both were treated as mere curiosities.

Until an outsider came along. It took a philosopher—a philosopher of morality and linguistics at that—to entirely change the field of IQ research. James Flynn, a persistent critic of mainstream IQ research from the 1970s onward, took the trouble to document just what the title of his most famous paper said: "Massive IQ Gains in 14 Nations."[3] On most kinds of IQ tests—whether Raven's or Wechsler, whether written or mostly spoken—there were big increases in average IQ scores in the long run in every country for which Flynn had data.

Years later, while writing their influential book *The Bell Curve*, political scientist Charles Murray and psychologist Richard Herrnstein called this long-term rise in IQ scores *The Flynn Effect*, and the name has appropriately stuck. A few researchers prefer to call it the Lynn-Flynn effect or even the FLynn effect (*sic*) since, as we saw, Lynn made his own contribution on the topic. But Flynn's systematic data collection and his decision to clearly point out that this rise in national IQs was strong evidence that the environment had a big impact on group IQ scores were the foundations for a revolution in IQ research. Once psychologists knew that these national IQ gains were big and were everywhere, the search for explanations began.

The Flynn Effect: The Fruit of Free Inquiry

Later work has shown that the IQ gains tended to be larger on tests that were more abstract and less concrete. According to Flynn, the biggest gains in the rich countries have been on Raven's-type matrix questions and on verbal similarities questions.[4] Flynn's example of a verbal similarities question is "What do dogs and rabbits have in common?" Both matrix and similarity questions involve drawing out abstractions in a concrete setting; both involve looking beyond what is right in front of you. Flynn himself believes that the rise in IQ scores reflects part of the "cognitive history of the 20th century," a time when modern life increased the demand for abstract thinking, when cultural and economic changes spurred children and adults alike to use their brains differently from in the past.[5] Flynn sees some possible role for nutrition and health improvements, but at least when discussing the Flynn Effect in rich countries, he prefers to discuss—in two fascinating books and elsewhere—how we humans are, on average, using our brains differently from how our ancestors did.[6]

Flynn's favored explanation for most of the Flynn Effect deserves our attention, but explanations by other scholars deserve attention as well. What are they saying? At this point, about three decades after the Flynn Effect was first conclusively documented, it's safe to say that there are too many explanations for it. At least a dozen stories have at least a patina of plausibility, each of which might explain a little or a lot of the overall IQ increase. But before turning to those stories, let's see what Flynn has had to say about the value of IQ research. Flynn is an enthusiastic supporter of academic freedom. He wants researchers to feel free to ask the most provocative of questions in the academic arena. As he has written more than once, the only reason he discovered the Flynn Effect is because he was trying to refute Berkeley psychologist Arthur Jensen's claim that IQ differences across demographic groups are difficult if not impossible to eliminate. Flynn wanted to refute the claim that environmental, cultural, and nutritional interventions to boost average group IQ are largely worthless. He was motivated by scientific controversy, and in his mind, his own discovery of rising IQ never would have occurred had IQ been too controversial to study. He needed grist for the scientific mill, and IQ researchers such as Jensen provided it for him. Thanks to their hypotheses we now know that massive IQ gains are possible for nations.

And Flynn himself believes that closing IQ gaps across demographic groups is important for achieving economic equality:

Flynn, a top official in New Zealand's left-of-center Alliance party, coauthored a paper in 2012 claiming,

> IQ is also important because some group differences are large and predictive of performance in many domains. Much evidence indicates that it would be difficult to overcome racial disadvantage if IQ differences could not be ameliorated. IQ tests help us to track the changes in intelligence of different groups and of entire nations and to measure the impact of interventions intended to improve intelligence.[7]

So Flynn and his coauthors believe raising IQ scores for "entire nations" is important for improving real-world outcomes. But Flynn laments the scarcity of research into the causes of group differences in test scores. In one of his recent books, after criticizing the theory that the Ice Age caused some human populations to evolve higher levels of intelligence, Flynn wrote,

> The collapse of the Ice Ages hypothesis does not, of course, settle the debate about whether there are racial differences for genes for intelligence. If universities have their way, the necessary research will never be done. They fund the most mundane research projects, but never seem to have funds to test for genetic differences between races. I tell US academics I can only assume that they believe that racial IQ differences have a genetic component, and fear what they might find.[8]

To close the gap in test scores across countries, it would be helpful to know *all* of the causes of the gap, and it would be helpful to be able to conclusively rule out some potential causes of the gap. But since research has only seriously explored a small number of potential causes, I will only discuss that shorter list. Perhaps future research will be able to provide a more comprehensive list, one that conclusively rules out, in Flynn's words, "racial differences for genes for intelligence."

Nutrition, Health, and IQ

Let's return to a question that might be possible to answer, the question of what causes the Flynn Effect. In fact there are if anything *too many* explanations for the Flynn Effect, an embarrassment of theories. And aside from a few short-run experiments, we overwhelmingly have to rely on mere observational studies: this or that particular trait has increased over time, and this or that trait sounds like it might help IQ, to the mind of a psychologist or a medical doctor, so we chalk that trait up as a possible driver of the Flynn Effect, and a possible path toward raising national average IQ around the world.

Let's first turn to a promising set of channels: nutrition and health. People in the rich countries are taller and healthier and longer-lived than their ancestors a century ago, and since the brain is part of the human body, it seems entirely plausible that the same forces making the rest of our bodies healthier are making our brains healthier as well. Fewer childhood diseases plus more nutritious and more stable sources of food add up to a strong *prima facie* case that body health and brain health traveled together over the past century. We've already started the chapter with one public health study on the topic, and in his textbook, psychologist N. J. Mackintosh points to studies showing that maternal alcohol abuse and (possibly) maternal smoking hurt a child's IQ throughout life.[9] But the evidence that overall maternal nutrition matters for a child's IQ is actually more mixed: while there is a well-documented relationship between low infant birth weight and low child IQ, it's as always difficult to know whether the birth weight itself—and maternal nutrition in particular—are causing the low child IQ.

In fact, there's some evidence that maternal nutrition might not matter much at all. The key evidence comes from the horrific experience of famine in the Netherlands during World War II. Some Dutch towns were cut off from regular food supplies toward the end of the war—daily calories were down to about one-third of the typical recommended levels at one point—and the children in gestation during that period had low birth weight. But when these children grew up, their IQs were nearly identical to those of children born a few years earlier or a few years later: massive *in utero* food deficiencies had no long-term effect on child IQ. This study has turned into a touchstone: it appears to prove that short-run food shortages *by themselves* aren't a major cause of low IQ.

But let's consider some evidence that the behavior of expectant mothers might matter after all. It's an admittedly speculative channel, just based on observation, not on experiments or the horrors of war: expectant mothers who regularly exercise tend to give birth to children with higher birth weights. Psychologist Richard Nisbett, in his clever book *Intelligence and How to Get It*, recommends that expectant mothers exercise partly because of this possible benefit, drawing on a fact we've already run across:

> The babies born to exercising mothers have larger heads. We know that people with larger brains are more intelligent on average.[10]

There's stronger evidence that maternal breast-feeding (for up to nine months) boosts a child's IQ by perhaps six points. The literature here is convoluted partly because reality is convoluted: whether or not breast-feeding boosts IQ appears to turn on the child's precise genetic makeup. Terabytes of bandwidth have been spent on medical debates over the value of breast-feeding on childhood brain development; because of the high interest in the topic, this is one area in which IQ research goes forward with little complaint. But remember: if IQ is "just a test score" with little real-life relevance, then of course it's probably not a good use of scarce resources to find out whether maternal exercise, maternal nutrition, or breast-feeding have large impacts on it. But if a nation's average IQ is an important driver of national prosperity, then further research is obviously needed to establish how much these or other health interventions matter for an infant's IQ.

Famines lasting a few months might not matter for a child's brain development. But what about chronic malnutrition among the young? And are there narrower, more targeted food deficiencies that might still matter for brain health? Here the evidence is stronger that policy matters, though perhaps it should be no surprise if an economist reports that the long run—chronic malnutrition—probably matters more than the short run—a horrible famine lasting a few weeks. As the debate between Lynn and Wicherts over sub-Saharan African IQ scores demonstrated, average IQs are lower in the poorest populations within a country, and surely the poorest populations are the most malnourished on average. But how much of these within-country IQ differences are directly due to malnutrition? Again, the experimental method offers an answer. In one study of Guatemalan villages, some malnourished children were given a protein supplement and some were given a nonprotein supplement, and then their cognitive skills were measured in few different ways. Of the two interventions, the protein supplement gave a bigger boost to student scores.[11]

This is the kind of on-the-ground research that needs to happen all the time, with multiple cognitive skill tests, to establish evidence-based human capital policy. Well-meaning development experts talk about the importance of "education," but as we saw in the Introduction, the evidence that extra education substantially boosts national prosperity is limited while the evidence that higher test scores boost national prosperity is stronger. Future human capital policy should be built around raising broad-based test scores. If boosting years of education helps in that goal, let's push to increase education. But if not, then let's focus on interventions that actually boost scores, interventions that might include protein supplements for chronically malnourished children.

But what if the mental stress of poverty itself is enough to lower test scores? Economists Sendil Mullainathan and Eldar Shafir ran experiments to find out just that. A review of their book, *Scarcity: Why Having Too Little Means So Much*, notes,

> Merely asking poorer people to contemplate a hypothetical £1,000 car repair, one study by the authors shows, impairs their performance on intelligence tests as much as missing a night's sleep—about 13 or 14 IQ points. In another study, Indian sugar cane farmers performed worse pre-harvest, when money was tight, compared to post-harvest. "Scarcity captures the mind," explain Mullainathan and Shafir.[12]

If Mullainathan and Shafir's hypothesis turns out to be far-reaching, then some poor countries may be trapped in a vicious cycle, a poverty trap, in which low cognitive skill means less productivity which creates more anxiety about poverty which keeps cognitive skills low and so on, endlessly. Their hypothesis, if true, could mean that a large, temporary gift to poor nations could help to break this cycle of despair, curb the anxiety, boost cognitive skills, and raise national productivity. Such a promising hypothesis—a sign that IQ matters for global poverty—certainly needs further testing.

Does Education Increase Intelligence?

People with more education tend to do better on IQ tests. How much of that is because schools train people to do well on tests? That's at least some of the explanation, but schooling gives a bigger boost to some measures of IQ than to others. Here, two IQ textbooks tell similar stories.[13] IQ is sometimes broken down into two "general" factors:

1. A "fluid intelligence" factor: the ability to solve new problems, sometimes measured by the Raven's matrices or a verbal similarities test, though reverse digit span (reciting a list of numbers in reverse order) appears to draw on the same ability.

2. A "crystallized intelligence" factor: the ability to recall old facts and old solutions to problems, sometimes measured by trivia tests and vocabulary tests.

So far it appears that schooling clearly boosts crystallized intelligence, but the typical effect of school on fluid intelligence may be small or even nonexistent. People can memorize facts, they can practice, and practice indeed gives individuals more facts to draw upon. But when it comes to solving new problems, formal training only goes so far and perhaps might not help at all.

Here are two examples of apparently successful increases in fluid intelligence. First, in a study in Sudan, a few months of training on the abacus appeared to boost Raven's matrix scores dramatically.[14] Second, a study of Israeli schoolchildren, comparing students of similar ages who were born just before or just after the school's age cutoff: because students who are born before the cutoff get an extra year of formal schooling, the age cutoff let the researchers identify the effect of an extra year of schooling on student IQ scores.[15] The researchers found a bigger effect on vocabulary scores than on matrix scores, but nevertheless matrix scores indeed rose for students who had received an extra year of schooling.

This pair of studies give a sense of a small but important literature that tries to answer a critical question for government policy: How does education change students? It's clear that education raises something called an "IQ score," but it matters whether that increase shows up in general problem-solving skill or merely in the ability to do well on a trivia test. The evidence, limited as it is, suggests that education may be able to boost general reasoning ability, at least in the short run, a result that would perhaps be no surprise to Flynn. In Flynn's view, the twentieth century was a time when life became more like an IQ test in the rich countries. Abstract reasoning, pulling facts out of their context and comparing them to other facts: these became valuable tools in our age of abstraction.

And school can be and often is a place where students are trained to think abstractly, systematically. A few hours a week of training in the classroom might help prepare some of the world's poorest students for the modern economy.

Perhaps—just perhaps—students need more abacuses in their schools. Practice with any tool of abstract reasoning may turn out to be vastly more important than studying history, learning to spell, or memorizing the definition of yet another polysyllabic word. If there are practical ways to boost fluid intelligence in the world's poor countries, we should make this a top priority for education policy. Then again, protein bars may turn out to be a more effective path to the same destination. Only time and a serious cost-benefit analysis will tell.

Do Those Around Us Shape Our Test Scores?

Among education researchers a recurring question is whether it's good for a student to be around higher-scoring students; that is, whether there are "peer effects" in the classroom. One prominent paper in the field, by Stanford's Caroline Hoxby, reminds us that peers might shape our learning in many ways:

> Although one channel for peer effects is students instructing one another, peer effects may also work through classroom disruption, changes in classroom atmosphere, or resources that some students bring with them from home.[16]

The question of whether other students shape a child's learning is one version of a broader question: Do our neighbors, our families, our friends shape who we are? Social scientists Christiakis and Fowler gave their answer in the title of their popular book, *Connected: How Your Friends' Friends' Friends Affect Everything You Feel, Think, or Do*.[17] In the case of classroom learning, the evidence is mixed on whether your child's standardized test scores will likely rise if she's in a classroom of high achievers or tend to fall if she's placed in a classroom of weaker students. This is one question that's been tested and retested in numerous ways in classrooms around the world, and perhaps the best way to summarize this vast literature is to say that some signs point to positive peer effects and some point to no peer effects at all. Amid the ambiguous findings, the clearest peer effect is that disruptive students hurt learning. As economists Burke and Sass report in their own study of peer effects,

> Despite the by now extensive list of papers that estimate peer effects of various stripes in academic settings, findings vary widely across studies, and consistent policy implications are hard to extract . . . [But] a handful of recent papers appear to show broad agreement that disruptive peer behavior has negative effects on individual achievement"[18]

Perhaps future research will clarify the situations in which peers matter for test scores, and whether those peer effects are lifelong rather than transitory. But until then the conservative position would be to take the average: a child's peers probably matter a little.

The Many Possible Sources of the Flynn Effect

Education and health are the two most concrete, policy-relevant explanations for the Flynn Effect, and they deserve the most attention. But there are other channels that might matter. Some might be hard to seriously investigate, and some might not offer policymakers practical levers that can boost national average IQ, but each are worth thinking about as a reminder of just how little social scientists know about this incredibly important topic. Each of these have been discussed in academic writings; none are my own ideas:[19]

> *"In raising the world's IQ, the secret's in the salt,"* stated an article in the *New York Times* in 2006. Iodine deficiency in some children

can hurt childhood brain development and push down adult IQ. Rich countries have tended to introduce iodine into the salt supply, quietly, helping to push up IQs around the world.[20]

More guessing on multiple choice questions: Some IQ tests such as the Raven's are *all* multiple choice, and unlike on the SAT there's no penalty for guessing incorrectly on an IQ test. In recent decades, students do appear to guess more often rather than leaving an item blank, so this could be part of the Flynn Effect—though only a small part, since IQ tests that aren't multiple choice show similar increases in scores.

Giving similar IQ tests to the same students: This is a practice effect. When you've seen one Raven's test you've pretty much seen them all: there's just one "Standard Progressive Matrices" test with just one set of questions. There's no thousand-question test bank that a psychologist can go to each time he wants to give the Raven's to a new group of students. Even other IQ tests typically only have a small number of versions, so students who take a few IQ tests in childhood—once when applying to a private school, once for a psychological evaluation, once for a scientific study—may end up taking exactly the same test more than once. Standardized testing is now standard, so if there really is such a thing as being a "good test taker" then more recent generations are more likely to have good test-taking skills—because of all the extra practice.

Smaller families, so more adult attention per child: There's some debate over the effect of family size on IQ, but in smaller families children typically receive more adult attention, are more likely to hear adults speaking to each other, and are more exposed to mature ways of thinking at an early age. More words, bigger words, more complex ideas: children from smaller families are likely to get all three. And that might boost IQ both on the test and perhaps even in the real world.

More indoor lighting: This is the most speculative of the channels listed here. With more artificial daylight there's more time to read, more time to look at symbols, and more time to analyze.

Flynn's theory: Life has become more like the IQ test: I've mentioned Flynn's theory before, and it bears repeating that it's "just a theory" and it's a theory that will be hard to test and perhaps even harder for a policymaker to use, but it's a theory too powerful to ignore. In Flynn's world, abstraction used to be a modestly useful skill while concrete, memorized, routinized skills—skills more like crystallized, factual intelligence—were more important and more practical. Today, abstraction is the skill most in demand, whether it's figuring out a new software program or thinking about how to drive on this familiar-but-unfamiliar interstate highway to deciding how to treat this stranger who is asking me if I'd like to order now. Looking for relationships between facts is a skill we use more often than we did before, according to Flynn, and so our mental maps are probably very different from the maps of most of our ancestors.

Much has been written on the Flynn Effect, most of it speculative, and I hope I haven't broken any new ground in the discussion here. The Flynn Effect proves that big IQ gains are possible, it strongly suggests that at least some of the IQ gains are in fluid reasoning skills that probably matter for a modern economy, and it offers the hope that nations with the lowest average scores can raise their scores through practical policy reforms. But the question of how much of the Flynn Effect is a real increase in key cognitive skills and how much is a merely nominal increase in narrow test-taking abilities is still an open one.

I close with a channel mentioned at the beginning of this chapter, a channel that might help to boost national average IQ, a channel that is concretely practical: lead abatement. It's a well-established fact that lead in the environment—in paint, in gasoline, in pipes, and in so many other places—lowers IQ. One time that it's always socially acceptable to discuss IQ research is when research demonstrates, once again, that environmental lead hurts IQ scores. One important study showed that at least in the United States environmental lead increased crime rates, and the same study also suggested that a substantial fraction of the recent decline in violent crime happened because Americans banned leaded gasoline, leaded paints, and other sources of lead exposure.[21] A key piece of evidence: some U.S. states imposed the rules earlier than other states, so one could check to see whether these early adopters saw their crime rates plunge earlier than other late adopters. And crime rates fell first among the early adopters. A study of lead abatement across multiple rich countries likewise found that less lead predicted less violent crime.[22] The pro-environmental policy of lead abatement may have had far-reaching consequences, pushing down murder rates while it boosted IQ scores, a policy apparently worth its cost many times over. Kevin Drum at *Mother Jones* notes a

> . . . growing body of research linking lead exposure in small children with a whole raft of complications later in life, including lower IQ, hyperactivity, behavioral problems, and learning disabilities.[23]

But lead exposure is still a real problem. Sub-Saharan Africa was the last major region of the world to eliminate lead from its gasoline, a goal that apparently was reached in 2006.[24] If lead really has been eliminated at long last from sub-Saharan African gasoline, then we can expect noticeably better brain health in that region over the next two decades. But surely lead exposure is still occurring in too many poor countries, and while major exposures might be relatively limited, the low-level, subclinical exposure is surely nudging down test scores across the developing world. If every IQ point matters, then every effort to reduce lead exposure matters as well. I close with the example of lead exposure partly because it's an example of a practical policy to boost national average IQ, and partly because it's a way to signal that with more research, I hope we'll find dozens of other policies that can successfully boost every nation's average IQ to the levels of the countries of East Asia.

Chapter 4

WILL THE INTELLIGENT INHERIT THE EARTH?

YOU'RE MADE AN OFFER BY A MAJOR EUROPEAN UNIVERSITY: 100 euros now versus a larger sum a year from now. The range of potential larger sums runs something like this: 102.5 euros, 105, 107.5, 110, and so on. You'll be handed a check right after the experiment, but the check will either be cashable today or postdated for a year from now. The people running the experiment will flip a coin to decide whether you get the 100 euros now or your larger, later choice, so you have every reason to give an honest answer because either option could really happen. How big does the larger sum have to be before you're willing to wait a year?

Some details aside, this is the experiment that economists Dohmen, Falk, Huffman, and Sunde ran on a thousand German adults a few years ago.[1] They also gave the test subjects parts of an IQ test. And they found something that many psychologists and economists have found before and since: people who get higher scores on an IQ test make more patient choices, so they don't have to be paid as much to wait. A fifteen-point rise in IQ predicted a shift of about 2.5 euros' worth of patience. The authors checked to see if the IQ-patience effect was just a side effect of education, or if it could be explained by family income or by whether the person was temporarily short on cash, or a few other factors. Those factors couldn't explain the link between IQ and patience. In this kind of experiment and many others, in test after test, people with higher scores on cognitive skill tests tend to wait. In psychology, this link between IQ and patience is uncontroversial—it turns up all the time. Yale psychologists Shamosh and Gray summarized over twenty studies and found a positive relationship, weak but real, between IQ and patience.[2] On average, smarter people are more patient.

One might speculate about the root causes. Is it mostly a story of patient children studying harder because they're patient, building up more cognitive skills over the years, or is it because kids with more cognitive skills are better able to imagine the future, to think of ways to keep the focus off of instant gratification? Speculation about the *why* is interesting, and perhaps soon we'll have answers to this question. But the *what*, the link between IQ and patience, is already there for all to see.

Economists tended to ignore this fact until a few years ago, when mainstream economists became much more interested in psychology. The new field of behavioral economics, at the intersection of psychology and economics, has drawn economists' attention to the obvious truth that people aren't the robotic, rational decision makers that textbook economic theory sometimes assumes. I've never seen much evidence that good economists really believed in the caricatures of super-rational *homo economicus*—Keynes, father of macroeconomics, placed a lot of weight on psychology, self-delusion, and human irrationality—but it's one thing to say "people aren't super-rational" and quite another to say "people are irrational in *this particular way*."

And the latter is what behavioral economics has allowed us to do. One of the big, robust results of behavioral economics is that many people are extremely impulsive in the very short run. They treat the difference between a dollar today and a dollar tomorrow as a massive deal, even though they treat the difference between a dollar in a week and a dollar in eight days as no big deal. *Right now versus tomorrow* is a massive difference. Economists have started calling this fact *hyperbolic discounting* of the future. Technically, *hyperbolic* refers to the hyperbola we learned about in algebra class—a steep curve—but I prefer to think of it as how dramatically, how hyperbolically, somebody reacts when they find out they'll have to wait to get their money.

This hyperbolic discounting shows up in brain scans. At the risk of oversimplification, the human brain's main decision centers fall into two regions: the limbic system (the lizard brain), close to your brain stem, and the prefrontal cortex, which is further to the front, right under your forehead. The limbic system responds emotionally, impulsively, and instinctively. When somebody is thinking about a candy bar *right in front of her eyes*, the limbic system lights up, eager with anticipation. That's the same part that lights up when a person is thinking about $1.00 today versus $1.50 tomorrow. And when the limbic system lights up, the person is extremely likely to choose instant gratification. But have that same person think about $1.00 in a week versus $1.50 in eight days, and the limbic system goes dark. Instead, the brain's energy is being spent in the cool, rational prefrontal cortex. That's *homo economicus* at her best: weighing the benefits against the costs, thinking through her options. She'll almost surely wait the extra day for the extra fifty cents.

So far, so good: sometimes people act rationally, sometimes they act impulsively. Behavioral economics matters. But economists Benjamin, Brown, and Shapiro went one step further.[3] The title of their paper asks a provocative question: "Who Is Behavioral?" They asked high school students in Chile to decide between money right now and money later, they gave them all IQ-type tests, and they found out that the students with lower IQs tended to take the money sooner. This relationship held true even if they took account of the fact that high-IQ students tended to have better-educated and richer parents. The authors also looked at U.S. survey data on who tends to smoke, who tends to have a savings or investment account of some sort, and who tends to have more assets than debts. Smoking is often considered an impulsive behavior, especially in a world in which we know the long-run health risks of smoking, and setting up a savings plan or keeping debts low and savings high requires some mix of cognitive skill and foresighted thinking. And the authors found something that's been found elsewhere: even if you know a person's income, even if you know a person's family background, knowing that person's IQ score helps you predict whether she smokes, whether she has more savings than debts, whether she has a savings or investment account at all. Cognitive tests predict foresighted behavior among children and among adults.

At least when it comes to impatience and impulsivity, behavioral economics applies especially to people with lower IQ scores. People with higher IQs, by contrast, are more likely to act like the rational *homo economicus* when faced with short-run temptation. And this finding that higher-scoring people tend to be less behavioral and more rational shows up elsewhere in economic experiments. One study found that people who did well on a short IQ-style test, the Cognitive Reflection Test, were less likely to make common mistakes in logical reasoning—both mistakes involving purely verbal logic and those that require people to think about probabilities.[4] Perhaps by now this is of little surprise—IQ helps predict verbal and math reasoning skills across the board—but when behavioral economists trumpet their findings of flawed human reasoning, it's worth keeping in mind that some of those flaws are less common among people who do well on standardized tests.

By now we've seen that there are numerous psychology and economics lab experiments and surveys showing that high-IQ people are more patient. But you might be reluctant to generalize from experiments and surveys: the experiments usually involve just a few dollars, perhaps $100 at most, and survey responses might be inaccurate. But in one unique case, the stakes were much higher and the financial questions weren't just a survey, they actually documented a major life choice. After the Cold War ended, the U.S. military was going to downsize, and so it decided to buy out members of the armed forces voluntarily. Enlisted personnel were offered an option: a lump sum of cash now worth an average of $25,000 versus a stream of payments over fifteen years that added up to much, much more than the lump sum.

And because it's the U.S. military, they had data on everything about the military personnel. So economists Warner and Pleeter went to work, trying to find out what kind of people took the annuity over the lump sum.[5] They threw in the kitchen sink: whether a person was an engineer, what his or her income was in previous years, gender and ethnic background, and many more factors. Even after knowing all of those facts, it turns out that the IQ test the personnel had taken long before helped predict whether they took the lump sum or the stream of payments. Of course, those with high IQs were more likely to take the stream of payments, the annuity. Facing this major life decision with thousands of dollars at stake, smarter enlistees were more patient. This is a finding worth remembering, since in economic theory and in real life, *patience really matters*.

Why Are Smarter People More Patient?

So often in social science, there's a yawning gap between knowing *that* something is true and knowing *why* it's true. The link between IQ and patience is a case in which multiple witnesses agree about *what* happened. But coming up with a good explanation for *why* it happened pulls us into a realm of storytelling and intuition, backed up once again by a few key facts. Shamosh and Gray claim that one reason higher IQ predicts great patience is because carefully considering the future requires the ability to keep multiple facts in mind simultaneously.[6] Let's consider their theory: if you have to decide between $100 today or $150 a year from now, you have to think about

1. The present situation with no extra money
2. The future situation with no extra money
3. How much your present situation might be improved by having that $100 right now
4. How much your future situation might be improved by having $150 a year from now

That's *four* facts to keep in mind to make just *one* decision between now versus later. If you're bad at keeping all of those facts in mind, you'll probably make a worse decision. And if there's one reliable result from IQ tests, it's that people with high IQs are better at keeping multiple facts in their head at once. One example is the IQ subtest known as "reverse digit span" mentioned earlier: it tests how many numbers you can repeat back to a psychologist, *while reversing the order in which he recited them to you*. So if he said 3, 1, 9, you answer 9, 1, 3. The longer the list you can recite error-free, the higher your score is likely to be on the other parts of the IQ test.

It turns out that reverse digit span is a better predictor of your overall IQ than forward digit span: memorizing long lists of numbers is hard, but memorizing them while also reversing their order in your mind is much harder. And people who can do that harder task tend to have more cognitive skills overall. So Shamosh and Gray conclude that IQ might cause patience because high IQ usually means an ability to juggle a lot of facts in one's head. And that's a skill that helps you weigh the benefits of waiting against the costs. The link between IQ and patience is so important that it certainly deserves more research. We know *that* the two go together—but we'd like to know even more about *why*.

And it's not just "juggling" that you're doing when you compare present and future in your mind: you're also *imagining* at least for a moment what it would be like to experience these different amounts of money at different points in time. Thinking of the future as a real place, with real consequences, means that for a few moments you need to live in Willy Wonka's "world of pure imagination."

Patience and Savings

Back in 1928, the legendary economist Frank Ramsey saw the link between patience and imagination: "Discount[ing] later enjoyments in comparison with earlier ones . . . arises merely from the failure of the imagination."[7] His "mathematical theory of saving" is built around that idea, and it's at the heart of modern macroeconomics. The "Ramsey growth model" shows that one way for a nation to get richer is for it to build up a bigger stock of machines and equipment—and the way to build up more machines and equipment is for the average citizen to put more of her paycheck in the bank rather than spend it on consumer goods. That way, the bank has money to lend to businesses, money that can be used to rent offices, buy computers and lab equipment, and keep a business up and running until it starts turning a profit.

This is the great and surprising equation at the heart of macroeconomics: savings equals investment. Much of macroeconomics involves spelling out just what that means. For instance, the equation reminds you that paying off your credit cards is really a form of saving, since you're building up wealth—and at the same time, you're handing money to a bank that can lend it to somebody else. The equation reminds you that things get a lot more complicated when you think about foreign countries—since one nation can pay for its new machines by borrowing the savings from another country. And finally, it reminds you that when all is said and done, the only way to build up about $30 trillion or so worth of machines and equipment and factories and offices—the amount that exists in the United States today—is for a lot of people to sacrifice today in the hopes of reaping rewards in the future. Investment demands patience. Economists had known this was true for centuries—but Ramsey wrote it in a few equations so simple and so beautiful that they created a minor revolution.

In the real world, IQ typically arrives bundled with patience, and patience causes savings, so you might think that high-IQ countries would tend to have higher savings rates. And you'd be right. Overall, as Figure 4.1 shows, the global relationship between a nation's average IQ and its national savings rate is moderately positive.[8] And this isn't just because higher-scoring countries have better-run governments that make it safer to save money: the national-IQ-to-national-savings relationship still holds when you take account of differences in the quality of each country's government. And the relationship would be even stronger if not for a few high-saving oil-rich coun-

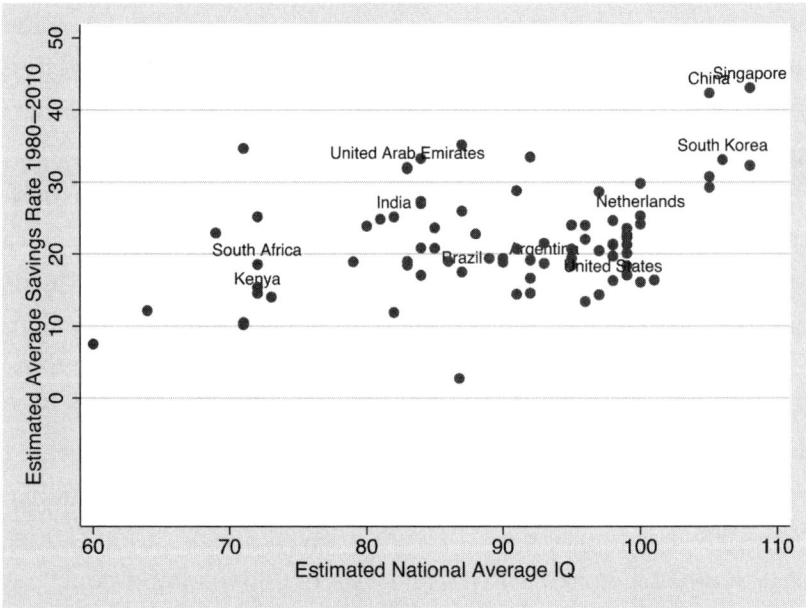

FIGURE 4.1 Estimated national average IQ and estimated national savings rates
Sources: Lynn and Meisenberg, "National IQs Calculated," and IMF World Economic Outlook's Gross National Savings Rate.

tries, nations that are perhaps saving for a future when their oil is gone. Higher-IQ countries are likely to be high-saving countries.

Of course, building factories and houses isn't the only way to save for the future. Getting an education is another way—you sacrifice time and money now in the hope of earning more cash later in life. And leaving natural resources for the future is another way to save: environmental degradation is a form of spending down national wealth. Do national average IQs predict the "genuine savings rate" of a nation, one that takes the environment and education into account?[9] Yes: again, even taking differences in national institutions into account, higher-scoring countries are more frugal; they tend to plan for the future.

Staying Frugal Like the Joneses

So high-IQ countries tend to save more—but are those savings rates just a sum of millions of personal decisions? Or is the hive mind at work? My colleague Bryan Caplan has often told me that the most important finding in sociology is that "people have a modest tendency for conformity." We tend to imitate what our neighbors are doing—maybe we just want to appear normal (imitating the average person) or maybe we want to "keep up with the Joneses" (by imitating people a little higher up in status) or maybe we want to learn the best way of doing things and so we look around in our society to find people worth imitating. A lot of this goes on subconsciously, to be sure: most people probably swear a little more around their high school friends than around their grandmothers, even if they're not consciously trying to conform.

In economics, the view that people's consumer spending habits are driven by social comparisons is often known as the *Veblen Effect* after the clever satirist, sociologist, and economist Thorstein Veblen. Veblen focused in particular on *conspicuous* consumption, on buying things that your neighbors can see, and buying items—or perhaps vacations to exotic locales—that demonstrate your social status. Cornell economist Robert Frank and Harvard economist Juliet Schor are modern proponents of the view that consumer spending is socially driven. And both say that our consumer decisions—to consume or to save, to work more hours a week or fewer—are deeply influenced by those around us. Our level of debt, our degree of frugality, our efforts to become prosperous, are all shaped by our environment. And our peers and our role models are part of our environment, shaping our consumer choices—a claim that is repeated in numerous college textbooks on consumer behavior.[10]

Here is one example of how spending and savings decisions are influenced by our neighbors. Did your neighbor win the lottery and buy a nicer car? That means that you're more likely to buy a nicer car too. At least that's what economist Peter Kuhn and his coauthors found when studying the results of lotteries in the Netherlands: people who won big lottery prizes tended to buy nicer cars (no surprise), but people who lived near the winners tended to buy nicer cars too.[11] Buying is a social activity: most of us try at least a little to fit in with our neighbors. You might think, "He's just talking about buying consumer goods—but his story is about saving, not consuming." But since consuming is the opposite of saving, people who buy more are saving less—unless perchance when the neighbor wins the lottery you decide to work just enough extra hours to pay for that nicer car. Personally I would welcome more patient neighbors, neighbors who could set an example of frugality, since it would make it that much easier for me to wait another year or two before getting a new roof or asphalting the driveway again. Frugal peers matter.

When the World Is Flat, the Frugal Inherit It

So far, I've followed Ramsey's original story: if your country saves more, then your country builds up a bigger capital stock. But don't some banks lend money to businesses in other countries? As a matter of fact, didn't a lot of banks in Asia and Europe lend money to U.S. homeowners in the run-up to the global financial crisis? Don't we live in a world of "hot money" and international investment banks and billions of yen and euros flashing across borders with the press of a button? Can we ignore these international capital flows so cavalierly?

One reason to ignore international capital flows, at least at first, is because once you add up the cash flowing in with the cash flowing out, the typical country's savings rate is a good measure of how much money is around to buy machines and equipment in that country. In other words, national savings is typically pretty close to national purchases of machines and equipment and buildings. Moreover, the link between the two is strong enough that it's a famous puzzle in international economics—the Feldstein-Horioka puzzle. Economists Feldstein and Horioka noticed that high-saving countries tended to have high capital purchases—even though simple economic models make an obvious point that savings should find its way around the world to the countries offering the best return on investment. And what were the chances of the frugal countries also being the best places to invest? Pretty small, in the eyes of most international economists. So the Feldstein-Horioka puzzle was born in 1980 and has fostered dozens of explanations. Most of these explanations involve some kind of imperfection in the financial markets—some reason why some savings ends up locked up in the country of origin. But regardless of the explanation, it appears that countries with high savings rates—which usually means countries with higher levels of patience—have more capital to invest at home and more equipment for workers to use. So "national savings equals national investment" isn't the place to end our thinking but it's a good place to start.

I tend to think that part of the explanation for the Feldstein-Horioka puzzle is that investment projects need some local money to get going.[12] So even when a multinational corporation with deep pockets decides it wants to open a new mining operation in a poorer, low-savings country, the multinational will still look around for some local help to show them the ropes, to make some key connections, to make a few phone calls and give advice on whom to hire. And the multinational is more likely to trust the local adviser if he can invest some cash into the project himself. The bigger the pool of high-saving locals, the more likely the multinational can find someone it can work with, someone it trusts, someone who can put skin in the game. More domestic savings probably means more multinational investment.

The net result: high-saving countries will tend to have more investment in machines, in factories, and in computers and software. And since these kinds of capital equipment tend to make workers more productive, the nation's output will tend to rise. Savings boosts investment boosts productivity boosts incomes. And since higher IQ predicts higher savings rates, the final outcome is that human capital tends to be abundant in the same countries where physical capital is abundant.

While the Feldstein-Horioka puzzle is real, it's also worth noting that whatever barriers to the global flow of capital exist today, they're probably going to be smaller in the future. As long as most countries keep integrating, average government quality keeps improving, and savings become ever-freer to flow across countries, the Feldstein-Horioka puzzle will become less and less of a puzzle each decade. And next we'll see that as the puzzle fades, the frugal literally will inherit the Earth.

Patience Is a Virtue

Economists have a sense of humor. When Harvard's Robert Barro and Columbia's Xavier Sala-i-Martin wrote their textbook *Economic Growth*, they put a Salvador Dali painting on the cover: melting trees, melting clocks, melting mountains.[13] It's a little bit crazy, like many of the best economic ideas.

The melting clocks are especially appropriate to this chapter. For patient people, time just seems to melt away, with the future feeling almost like the present. For the impatient, worrying about the future seems as unrealistic as any abstract painting: impatient people seize the day, *carpe diem*, they give no thought for the morrow. And these two views of time sum up Barro and Sala-i-Martin's big idea about patience in a world in which money flows freely across borders.

Let's take their model, their parable, their most extreme case, and walk through it for a moment. It takes Frank Ramsey's basic model, in which savings equals investment equals capital growth, and extends it to a world in which capital can flow freely around the globe to wherever it earns the most interest. They show that if savings can flow across countries to wherever the interest rate is highest, and if people can borrow across countries without trouble (say, by mortgaging their home to a bank that borrows money from investors in Japan), then in the long run there's only one possible outcome: *the most patient country owns everything*. The most patient country owns all of the capital equipment in the world, all of the shares of stock, all of the government bonds, all of the mortgages, everything. What happens in all of the other countries? Eventually, they spend essentially all of their national income repaying debt to the most patient country. They literally mortgage their future through decades of high living, decades during which they borrow cheap money that is gladly lent by more patient countries.

Let's look at how they got there. During the borrowing times, the less patient countries—let's just call them the Impatients—were glad to borrow: after all, they were borrowing money at, for example, 3 percent annual interest. Who could pass up a deal like that? You'd have to be a fool not to borrow all you could. If the interest rate had been 6 or 7 percent, things would've been different—the Impatients wouldn't have borrowed nearly as much, and might have only mortgaged a third or a half of their future.

But instead, with the low rates, the Impatients lived beyond their means, consuming more than their incomes.

But eventually the patient country decided to turn off the spigot. Why? Because the patient countries—the Patients—did the math, and figured out that if they lent any more, they wouldn't get repaid. The goal of lending is, of course, to get paid back at some point. So lenders tend to keep an eye on whether the borrowers are in a solid financial position. Eventually, borrowers get to a point where they start having to repay debt. After years of enjoying a grand life of consumption, the average Impatient eventually ends up spending its whole income on interest payments, forever. And those interest payments head right back to the most patient country. You might think, "That's just *money* Barro and Sala-i-Martin are talking about, not real goods and services." A reasonable thought, but here real goods and services are in play. During the borrowing times, the patient country was exporting endless supplies of cars and movies and clothing to the less-patient countries, but after the patient country stops lending, the flow will reverse: the exports will head from the Impatients back to the patient country. After all, that was why the patient country lent money, wasn't it? They wanted to eventually get something back from the countries they were lending to. The frugal inherited the Earth, and now they're going to enjoy it.

An extreme tale, surely, but Barro and Sala-i-Martin spell it all out in elegant mathematics. And underneath it is a simple story that we see in the lives of our friends and in the fates of nations: impatient people borrow a lot to consume when they're young and middle-aged, and it usually means that when they get old, they end up with little wealth and a lot of credit card debt, mortgaged to the hilt, and spending their twilight years eating bologna sandwiches and pirating their neighbor's wi-fi.

Of course, in the real world, we wouldn't expect there to be *exactly* one country owning *all* of the rest of the world's financial assets, but we'd certainly expect the most patient countries to own more than their share of the world's globally tradable investments. Further, not everything can be mortgaged to more patient countries, an obvious enough point, so the patient countries will only lend to the extent they can be reasonably confident of getting repaid. It's still up for debate just how freely money flows around the planet: people seem to own far too many stocks and bonds issued by businesses in their home country, a fact known as "home country bias." So globalization seems to be moving a bit slowly on the financial side—and that means we won't expect the real world to perfectly match the data . . . but we'd at least expect that in today's world, with money moving around the globe, the most patient countries will have more overseas investments than the less patient countries.

Do the data support the theory? Drawing on the massive data collection project of economists Philip Lane and Gian Maria Milesi-Ferretti, I found that when you look at each nation's holdings of *all* types of foreign investments, the high-average-IQ countries tend to be the heavyweights.[14] Net foreign wealth as a fraction of a nation's income is higher in higher-scoring counties. This has become even truer since the early 1970s, when capital started flowing more freely around the world. The high-average-IQ countries hold more foreign investments: more foreign stocks, foreign bonds, and foreign cash. They just save more global wealth.[15] And it's not just because the high-IQ countries have better governments or because they have higher incomes already. In my research I've already checked out those possibilities, and they can't explain the whole relationship. The countries filled with more gratification-delayers pile up quite a lot of future gratification. And because this trend has become stronger since the 1970s, it seems we're moving to a situation that looks more and more like Barro and Sala-i-Martin's equations, a world in which the most patient nations inherit quite a bit of the Earth.

Which nations are likely to be among the inheritors? A 2010 study published by two economists at the Congressional Budget Office states,

> It is well known that countries in East Asia—namely, Japan, South Korea, Taiwan, China, Hong Kong, and Singapore—on average have a higher national saving rate than do other regions. . . . Some analysts attribute this to East Asian's (*sic*) cultural factors, while others attribute it to the "East Asian growth model" which includes various policies designed to promote growth through capital accumulation, by making credit cheaper and more accessible to industries than to consumers.[16]

Economists Hung and Qian attempt to explain China's high savings rate through the typical economic channels—fast economic growth, a young population, rapid urbanization, for instance—but nevertheless find that those can't entirely explain the frugality. There's still what they call a "being an East Asian country" effect, and while the statistical tests don't unambiguously support the existence of a "being an East Asian country" effect, the results are strong enough that the authors wrestle with the question of just why that region has such high savings rates. Ultimately they conclude,

> Our results also suggest that some factors shared by East Asian economies have contributed to China's higher saving rate, and that those factors are mainly those underlying the high-savings-high-growth strategy of East Asian economies. However, it is beyond the scope of this paper to disentangle the many complex factors. . . .[17]

While there are many fascinating factors at work in the modern economic miracles of East Asia, may I submit one little-explored channel that deserves more attention: the entirely conventional relationship, documented repeatedly across the social sciences, between test scores and patience. As long as East Asia's test scores remain the highest in the world, it's quite likely that East Asian countries will continue to accumulate net assets the world over, providing investment funds for nations in search of cash.

A Large Debt Produces an Enemy

The economic benefits of borrowing are straightforward: if you're being offered cheap money and you've got a promising project, then it's great to have frugal neighbors to borrow from. But the long-run effects, economic and political, are worth thinking about since they're likely to shape the twenty-first century. First, let's consider the simple economics, ignoring the political side, and let's return to the basic story of two types of countries, those filled with Patients and Impatients. Just as your parents taught you, it's better to be patient than impatient—that much should be obvious. And future generations living in impatient countries are going to be quite disappointed when they become adults and realize that one-third or more of their tax money is used to send interest payments overseas. They'll also be disappointed that their parents have few assets to pass on, since the family home is mortgaged and the parents have spent down most of their retirement savings. It's easy to predict that some of these high-debt, impatient countries will default, and it's equally easy to predict that the most patient nations will anticipate those defaults—so the Patients will tend to cut back on lending well before default happens.

The Patients will also look for innovative ways to make sure their loans get repaid—one can just imagine the possibilities, from electronic holds on global cash flows to military invasions to everything in between. It will often be ugly, perhaps terrifying. As the Roman author Syrus said, "A small debt produces a debtor; a large debt, an enemy."

Which brings us to the political side of international debt. My colleagues and I sometimes play a board game called *Imperial*. It's a global strategy game, a lot like *Risk*, with one exception: instead of controlling the nations directly, you're an investment banker who holds the debt of different countries. And if you hold more of a given country's debt than any other player, you control that country. It's hidden control, to be sure—which makes the game all the more interesting. There was even a *Saturday Night Live* sketch about the power of debtholders in 2009: President Obama meets with Chinese Premier Wen Jiabao, and the premier keeps telling Obama how to run the country. Of course, the president has to listen since the Chinese government and its banks hold so much U.S. debt. You have to listen to your lender.

Is that how the real world works? Do debt-laden countries lose some control to their foreign investors? Yes, of course they do, *especially if they want to borrow again*. Those italics contain an important caveat: if you know your country doesn't want to borrow ever again—and if we stick with the mostly realistic assumption that investors can't sent a flotilla of ships or an army of attorneys to force repayment—it's typically a great idea to default on your debt. Your conscience may bother you, but that can be fixed with a couple of stiff drinks. And once you sober up, you'll have a lot more cash left to spend every month. This is a point that I remind my students of: countries don't often try to force other countries to repay debt anymore. And because of that fact, it's really the *borrower* who has the power in the relationship, not the lender. If the borrower repays, it's because it thinks it needs a good reputation—it wants to keep its country's credit score high.

Debt as a Commitment to Try

And that brings us to why countries—high-average-IQ, low-average-IQ, and in-between—might actually want to run up massive international debts: it's a way to commit to having a strong economy in the future. This may sound absurd, but corporations seem to do this all the time. Financial economist Michael Jensen wrote a Nobel-deserving paper on the topic.[18] He thought that one of the big problems with corporations is that stockholders don't trust CEOs: greedy stockholders care about the company's profitability while CEOs often just want the easy life and the regular paycheck. Stockholders want the company to run high profits for decades, but they have to rely on the CEO and her minions, who might just write annual reports saying, "We tried to run a bigger profit but it didn't work out; let's have next year's shareholder meeting in a nicer city."

What can the shareholders do to ensure that the CEO tries harder to maximize profits? They can force the CEO to issue debt, so that the CEO has to make big, regular interest payments every month. That way, the CEO lives with the fear of God in her heart: she knows if she misses an interest payment, the company goes into bankruptcy, and it'll be off with her head, a job lost, a reputation ruined. And that's just the kind of fear the shareholders want. The shareholders use debt to get the CEO to commit to run big profits, to be productive, to keep revenues high and costs low.

The same could be going on in national governments, even if only accidentally. By having outsiders—lenders from more patient countries—holding a nation's debt, governments are committing to having some outside monitor keep a sharp eye on the economy and make, well, *suggestions* for improvement from time to time. A bit like in the *Saturday Night Live* sketch, the monitor might demand that the indebted nation change its economic policies before getting any more loans.[19] If your nation is going to owe money to someone, it's best to owe money to someone who'd do a good job shaping your country's economic policies.

As we'll see later, IQ does correlate not only with patience but also with pro-market attitudes, so having lenders from countries with higher test scores will likely give a nation relatively pro-market lenders. By running a big debt, the Impatients may be outsourcing part of their economic policies to nations who are better at shaping economic policy. That's a possible side effect worth keeping in mind.

IQ, Patience, and Cooperation

In lab experiments, people who do better on IQ tests are usually more patient, and Ramsey's "mathematical theory of saving" predicts that people who are more patient save more. If you believe those two links in the chain, then you should connect them. When we look across countries, we see that, indeed, countries with higher average test scores have higher savings rates and are acquiring ever more of the world's assets. So far, the pieces of the story hold together.

But the Patients aren't just interested in putting some extra money in the bank: they care more about the future in *all* its forms. That means the Patients likely care more about their long-run reputation than people who seize the day. Imagine two societies: one in which the future feels like a dim shadow, the other in which the future seems as real as now. Which society will have more restaurants that care about repeat customers? Which society will have more politicians who turn down bribes because they worry about eventually getting caught?

In the next chapter, we'll see that in experiment after experiment, the intelligent act more like good citizens. And the link between IQ and patience helps to explain why.

Chapter 5

SMARTER GROUPS ARE MORE COOPERATIVE

> The ability to recognize the other player from past interactions, and to remember the relevant features of those interactions, is necessary to sustain cooperation.
> **ROBERT AXELROD, *THE EVOLUTION OF COOPERATION*** [1]

WE HUMANS ARE A SOCIAL SPECIES: we rely on each other to get things done. Whether it's building a car, creating a happy marriage, or holding a potluck dinner at church, we usually need to cooperate in order to achieve the big successes in life. But cooperation is hard. Economics professor Paul Seabright makes this point in his excellent book, *The Company of Strangers:*

> Nowhere else in nature do unrelated members of the same species—genetic rivals incited by instinct and history to fight one another—cooperate on projects of such complexity and requiring such a high degree of mutual trust as in the human species.[2]

Why is cooperation so hard? Because cooperating is often against your own best interest. When you're going to a potluck dinner, the smart thing to do is to bring a bag of chips while sampling other people's delicious casseroles. At some point before you arrive, you might think, "If *everyone* does that, then all we'll have at the potluck is twenty bags of chips." And that's true enough, but you have no influence over whether those other nineteen people bring chips or casseroles, so why not do what's best for yourself: chips it is.

This is one example of the famous "prisoner's dilemma," in which individual greed leads to an awful group outcome. Prisoner's dilemmas are everywhere, and they're the precise opposite of Adam Smith's famous "invisible hand," in which individual greed leads to a positive group outcome. Invisible hands and prisoner's dilemmas are both at work in the world: sometimes, as Gordon Gekko said in the movie *Wall Street*, "Greed is good," and sometimes greed creates misery. In this and the next chapter, we'll see how greed can create misery, and we'll see how higher-IQ groups are just a bit more likely to find a way to cooperate, a bit more likely to avoid the prisoner's dilemma.

The Real Prisoner's Dilemma

First off, let's go back to the source—the classic economic example of when greed is bad. You and your accomplice rob a bank, and a few hours later, you both get picked up by the police and put into separate interrogation rooms. The cops offer you a deal: if you cooperate and rat out your accomplice while your accomplice keeps her mouth shut, you'll get to walk and she'll get ten years. But the opposite is also true: If she talks and you're quiet, *you'll* get the ten years and she walks. Now, if you both talk, there'll be enough evidence that the cops will put you both away for five years. And if you both keep your mouths shut, the cops put you both away for a year on a minor weapons possession charge.

So, what's the rational thing to do? Well, if you think your accomplice will talk, you're facing a choice between ten years if you're quiet and five years if you talk. Five is less than ten, so the thing to do is spill the beans. And if you think your accomplice will be loyal to you, so she'll keep her mouth shut, then you get to walk free if you sing like a canary and you get one year if you keep quiet. Zero is less than one, so you talk. So *regardless* of what you think your accomplice will do, the right thing to do, the greedy thing to do, is to talk. Easy choice, right? Yes, it is. But just remember: your accomplice got the same deal. So she's going to make the same decision: she's going to talk and you're going to talk and you're both going to get five years in prison. A grim outcome.

Note that this prisoner's dilemma essentially is the same situation as the church potluck: regardless of what the other people are doing, the right thing for me to do is to try to get the best deal I can. And here we see the problem: if everyone just goes ahead and acts in his or her own individual best interest, we get an awful outcome. It's something students and office workers see on team projects: people just try to coast by on the efforts of others. They know that work is hard, and that any one person's effort isn't going to do that much to change the outcome. Any time many people are making a decision when each person's sacrifice mostly helps the others, then you're in a prisoner's dilemma. And doesn't that sound like a lot of modern life? Consider two more examples from the field of politics. A politician steers government funds to his supporters: What could be more rational? Or a politician spends his time on cable news, building up a national reputation as a radical reformer rather than quietly supporting a practical reform that might actually get enacted. In both cases self-interest drives the outcome. The rationality of pursuing self-interest even when it hurts society is precisely what makes reasonably fair, even-handed political outcomes such a puzzle. When short-run self-interest naturally leads to awful outcomes, it's a wonder that we ever see good political outcomes.

I'll save most of the political implications for the next chapter. For now, think about a married couple's decision to be sexually exclusive, to be faithful. Notice—I just treated it as if it were a group decision—the couple's decision—but groups can't make decisions, only individuals can. Let's be conventional, and think of this as a heterosexual married couple, since it makes it easier to follow the story with pronouns. The man is trying to decide whether to be faithful or cheat. The woman is facing the same decision. For the moment, we'll think of this as a one-time decision: a decision to choose cheating as a lifestyle. The best outcome for the man is for him to cheat while his wife is faithful. The best outcome for the woman is the reverse: she has the occasional fling while her husband stays at home playing video games every night. Now, what if the husband thinks his wife is cheating? Well, if it was a good idea for him to cheat when she was faithful, it's even a better idea for him to cheat if she's gallivanting around town, like the heartbreaker in a country song. So whether she's faithful or not, the best decision for the husband is to cheat—and we're back in the prisoner's dilemma.

If deciding whether to be faithful to your spouse is a once-and-for-all decision, the best strategy is clear: cheat. Yet in real life, people don't cheat all that often. Most marriages in rich countries are fairly monogamous—perhaps half of married couples cheat over decades of being together. But that means that half of married couples don't cheat—and even when marriages do involve infidelity, the affairs largely are short term. It's far from the everyday cheating you'd expect from our simple story that indicates, rationally, that everyone should cheat whenever possible.

Part of the reason there's so little cheating may be because divorce can be expensive, or because lots of spouses try to cheat, but can't find any willing partners. Nevertheless, there's an enormous amount of cooperation within marriages, there are a lot of people who pick up their neighbor's mail while they're on vacation, there are lots of people who bring casseroles to church potlucks—all without anybody really forcing anyone else to be kind. Why does this happen? One classic explanation is that life is what economists call a *repeated game*. And when the same two people play the prisoner's dilemma game again and again, whether in a college laboratory or in the halls of Congress, something magical happens: pairs of players often learn to cooperate. Not always and not reliably, but many people do decide to take the ABBA song to heart and "take a chance" on trust, on bringing the casserole this week, on staying faithful this year. And sometimes it works out just fine.

Deciding to trust doesn't mean acting naive: trust can be deeply shrewd. That's because if you know you're going to be playing the same prisoner's dilemma game with the same partner every week (at the church potluck) or every year (deciding whether to have that fling during the annual sales meeting), then the game looks very different. All of a sudden, both you and your partner have a way to punish each other: if you're mean to me this time around, I can be mean to you the next time around. As you give, so shall you receive; or as we usually put it, "tit for tat." So I'll take out the garbage as long as you do the dishes, but if you stop doing the dishes, I'll let the garbage pile up. And if you start doing dishes again, I'll go back to taking out the trash quickly. This kind of tacit cooperation is everywhere in personal relationships, in work relationships, in the neighborhood, and we take it for granted. Often enough, we're nice because everyone else is making it easy to be nice.

Economists figured this out in the early days of the field known as "game theory," that once you turn a one-shot prisoner's dilemma into a repeated game, it's possible for selfish players to rationally cooperate with each other, not out of a sense of generosity but out of pure self-interest. This result—that repetition can turn lemons into lemonade—is known as the "folk theorem." That's because it seemed fairly obvious once people started thinking about it, and no one economist was really willing to take credit for the idea.

One researcher—a political scientist, Robert Axelrod—went further than this. He saw repeated prisoner's dilemmas (RPDs) everywhere in politics and society, and so he concluded that if he could find out how to get people cooperating rather than descending into bitter defection, he could help make the world a more peaceful place. It sounds a bit naive—but it was nothing of the sort. Axelrod's research, summed up in his excellent book *The Evolution of Cooperation*, is still used by peace negotiators, labor-management mediators, and nuclear arms reduction experts.[3] His is an agenda that has made the world a better, safer place. And it began by just taking the repeated prisoner's dilemma seriously, so seriously that Axelrod decided to get a lot of social scientists together to play some games.

Axelrod ran a competition—not in real life, but on some 1970s-era computers. He invited social scientists, mathematicians, anyone interested to submit a simple computer program giving instructions to one of the electronic "players" in a two-person repeated prisoner's dilemma game. The winner of the tournament would be the contestant whose program could win the most points when pitted against the other computer programs. The most points, naturally, clocked in when the other player cooperated while you defected; when both cooperated you got a good outcome, but not as good as when you were exploiting the other player.

So dozens of researchers proposed dozens of computer programs for the tournament. As you can imagine, some programs were quite sophisticated, looking for ways to dupe the other computerized player into cooperating so that the entrant could exploit his partner for at least a few rounds of the tournament. But not every program was sophisticated; in fact one program followed the simplest rule possible: "always cooperate." Which computer program—which strategy—won the entire tournament? It's known by the phrase I mentioned earlier: *tit for tat*.

It plays out something like this. In the first round, I'll cooperate. After that, I just do whatever you did last time. So if you cooperated, then I'll take a chance on cooperation: I'll return good for good. If you defected, then I'll return evil for evil: I'll defect this time. But if you go back to cooperating, I'll forget about your unfaithfulness, and I'll go back to cooperating too. This simple strategy works well for many reasons, but three stand out. First, it opens the door to endless cooperation—and endless periods of decent-but-not-exciting rewards, just like most happy, faithful marriages. But second, it doesn't leave you open to the possibility of endless exploitation. Unlike some long-suffering spouses you may know, a tit-for-tat player punishes defection swiftly and smartly. And third, the punishment ends as soon as kindness returns: if your partner mends his ways, you forgive and forget. Grudges are for the petty.

Tit for tat combines an open right hand with an armed left hand.[4] In a society filled with tit for tatters, people would always cooperate, not because those people were doormats or naifs, but because any potential cheater would know that she would be quickly punished. So, tit for tat is a good strategy—something worth keeping in mind the next time you have an argument with the neighbors over who should fix the broken fence. But Axelrod wanted to do more than just pinpoint a good computer program: he tried to distill the essence of what made tit for tat and a few similar strategies work so well in order to convey those lessons to the world. He came up with some principles for encouraging cooperation in repeated prisoner's dilemma settings. Three of them matter for us: think of them as the *Three P's of the RPD*. Players should

1. Be *patient:* Focus on the long-term benefits of finding a way to cooperate—don't just focus on the short-run pleasures, whether it's the pleasure of exploitation or the pleasure of punishment. Axelrod calls this "extending the shadow of the future."
2. Be *pleasant:* Start off nice—make sure those bared teeth are part of a smile. And later in the game, take the ABBA approach, and take a chance on cooperating every now and then, even when things have gone south for a while.
3. Be *perceptive:* Figure out what game you're playing—know the rules, and know the benefits and costs of cooperation.

I claim that people with higher IQs will be better at all three. That higher-IQ players tend to follow the third piece of advice, "Be perceptive," is almost obvious: higher-IQ individuals are just more likely to *get it*, to *grok* the key ideas, as sci-fi writer Robert Heinlein used to say. Not always, not perfectly, but as we saw in the coda to Chapter 1, on average individuals with high IQ are better at grokking the rules of the social game, they're more socially intelligent. And as we saw in the last chapter, IQ also tends to predict patient behavior. Those who see the patterns in the Raven's Progressive Matrices also see the future. That means that in a repeated prisoner's dilemma, they'll tend to focus on the rewards of long-term cooperation, not the short-term thrills of punishment or exploitation.

My final claim is that higher-IQ people are nicer than most other people—at least when they're in settings such as the repeated prisoner's dilemma. Can that really be the case? You might expect higher-IQ people to be a little meaner in some cases—they might try to exploit people if they figure out a way to exploit them. That might be important in some settings, but there are three interesting new experiments that show how high IQ predicts generosity.

Economist Aldo Rustichini and his coauthors gave IQ tests to a thousand people enrolled in a truck-driving school, and then they had them play a trust game.[5] A typical trust game—first invented by my George Mason colleague Kevin McCabe and his coauthors—works like this. The game has just two players, each making one choice. They can't see each other, and they never know who they're actually playing; in most cases, they're just facing a computer terminal. First, Player 1 starts with $5; he then decides how much of his money (if any!) to send to Player 2 and how much to keep for himself. If some of the money is sent over, the money sent magically triples in value. So if Player 1 sent over $2, Player 2 now has $6. Player 2 now gets to decide how much money to return to Player 1; she can return nothing and keep all $6, she can return all $6 and keep nothing for herself, or she can do something in between. Since McCabe and coauthors invented this experiment, it's been run numerous times: most players return just about the amount that Player 1 sent over—in other words, the average person is trustworthy, but no philanthropist.

Most people are interested in the question of "Who reciprocates? Who is trustworthy?" But here we're interested not in Player 2 but in Player 1: Who's the biggest sucker? Who takes the chance on sending money over—without a formal contract, without being able to even *see* the other person? Wouldn't we expect players with lower IQ scores to naively send over cash, in the hope that Player 2 will be generous? Wouldn't we expect a higher-IQ Player 1 to figure out that Player 2 has no incentive to be kind? We might, but in fact, Rustichini found just the opposite: the higher-IQ students in truck-driving school sent over more money than their classmates with lower IQs. So smarter players are more likely to start off by playing nice. This result—that IQ predicts "generous" or "nice" behavior—was backed up by a German study, a team-effort problem: a few players are each given a few Euros, and they each have to decide how much to chip in to the pot.[6] If the total amount chipped in is greater than, say, 10€, then the pot doubles, and the amount in the pot is split equally between all the players; if not, the pot evaporates, with nobody getting anything except the money they held out of the pot. In this study, higher-IQ players put more into the pot. They may have done it out of kindness to others, or they may have done it because they shrewdly calculated that they had a decent chance of being the donor who pushed the pot over the 10€ threshold, so it's hard to tell what their motives were. But in any case, smarter players chipped in more, and what they chipped in helped everyone in the group. They were more *pleasant*.

As a side note, Rustichini's truck-driver study also looked at Player 2's behavior: they checked to see if higher-IQ players were more trustworthy or less trustworthy than average. Compared to the average player, higher-IQ players were more likely to *reciprocate*. In other words, higher-IQ players were more likely to return good for good, evil for evil. That means that, in this experiment, higher-IQ players were the enforcers. They enforced the norm of reciprocity even when it cost money to do so.

Another study by Brown University economist Louis Putterman and his coauthors found still more evidence that higher-IQ individuals are more likely to start off by playing nice, by being generous team players.[7] In this game, known as the public goods game, players individually decide how much of their own money to put in a metaphorical pot, the money doubles or triples, and then it gets divided up among the group. When you give money, you're directly contributing to the public good. The game was repeated for a few rounds with the same team so players would have a chance to learn from each other, a chance to find a path to cooperation.

As this was run at Brown University, an Ivy League school where one might expect that almost all students are raised in incredibly advantaged environments, it might seem that differences in IQ scores would be irrelevant. But in Putterman's cooperation experiment, IQ mattered. He and his coauthors found that higher-IQ students at Brown put more money in the pot during the early rounds of the game: the higher-IQ students were more pleasant early on. That's the smart thing to do, because extra money early on can send a signal of kindness, of cooperativeness, to the other players. And it's worth noting that in another part of the experiment, when the students could vote on a way to penalize low contributors, higher-IQ students were more likely to vote for a rule that would penalize the non-cooperators: so higher-IQ students were pleasant, but not naive.

Intelligence as a Way to Read the Minds of Others

So people with higher test scores tend to have more of the Three P's of the RPD. But just how socially perceptive are higher-IQ people? After all, being nice in a lab experiment might not translate into real-world social interactions, and while IQ predicts social intelligence in surveys, it would be good to have a concrete test of social perceptiveness. One test by economist David Cesarini and his coauthors illustrates the ability of higher-IQ individuals to understand the minds of others.[8] The Keynesian Beauty Contest, as it is known, is a game in which all the players are asked to pick a number from zero to one hundred. A prize will be given to the person whose guess is closest to, say, one-half of the group's average guess. In the event of a tie they might split the prize among the best guesses. So if almost everyone chose fifty but just one person chose thirty, that lower guess would win. If the players were all perfectly rational, and they knew that everyone else in the game was equally rational, they would realize that the winning answer would be the only number that is exactly one half of itself: zero.

But people aren't perfectly rational and—here's the good part—people who are more rational are more likely to be aware of just how irrational most people are. So while the weaker players would pick numbers close to randomly—guessing on average fifty or a little below—someone better-skilled might realize that the group combines some sharper players with some weaker players, and so submit a guess quite a bit lower than fifty. But isn't there a chance that higher-IQ players make the mistake of thinking that everyone is as smart as they are? Or might they overthink the situation, foolishly submitting zero as the right answer? In a study of Swedes, Cesarini and coauthors found that players with the highest IQs submitted numbers that were low but not too low; indeed they gave answers that were strikingly close to the best possible answer. By contrast, players in the bottom of the IQ distribution gave answers that tended to be far too high. IQ predicted not just individual rationality but a better view into the minds of others. And later a second study came to the same finding using another IQ-type test.[9]

Overall, mental test scores predict the ability to understand the minds of others. And you might wonder: Why is it called the Keynesian Beauty Contest? It's based on a story the legendary economist John Maynard Keynes once told. A British newspaper published photos of women and had an accompanying contest:

the winners would be the contestants who chose the photo that was most often selected by everyone else. So while at first glance you might think it's a game of "pick the prettiest woman," the real goal is instead "pick the woman that I think everyone else will be picking." Keynes thought this was a useful metaphor for the stock market: while it seems prudent at first to invest in companies with strong objective prospects, Keynes thought the real game was in picking the companies that everyone else was soon going to be picking. Keynes believed that reading the crowd drew on a cognitively demanding skill: skill at understanding other humans.

High-SAT Schools and Cooperation

Axelrod pointed out three paths to cooperation—patience, pleasantness, and perceptiveness—and we've seen that higher-IQ people tend to follow all three pieces of advice in experimental settings. But wouldn't it be nice if there were some actual *evidence* that high-intelligence groups cooperate more often in a *genuine* repeated prisoner's dilemma? That's what I thought to myself in 2004, when I first started thinking about the link between repeated games, IQ, and productivity. I looked through the vast literature on repeated prisoner's dilemmas, trying to see if someone, somewhere, had run a repeated game and then given the players an IQ test—or even asked for the students' SAT scores. I found almost nothing.

But I did eventually find one exception: one study had twins play a repeated prisoner's dilemma game against each other for a hundred rounds, and they found that higher-IQ pairs of twins did cooperate more often than lower-IQ pairs of twins.[10] This was one piece of evidence that higher-IQ people cooperate more, indeed. But, since people were knowingly playing against their own siblings, I was reluctant to generalize to society at large.

Since I wasn't in a position to run my own experiments at the time, I instead began a program of collecting academic articles on dozens of repeated prisoner's dilemma experiments run at different U.S. universities.[11] The plan was simple: record the average rate of cooperation in each study along with a few other experimental characteristics—whether they played for cash, how many rounds the games lasted, whether the school was public or private, and so on. Then, record the average SAT score at that school both in the 1960s and the early 1970s (when most of these experiments were run, but when few schools reported average SAT scores) and today (when more data were publicly available).

The results? Students at schools with high average SAT scores cooperated more often than students at low-SAT schools. The relationship was between modest and strong, and the relationship still held, though not quite as strongly, when you took account of the fact that some schools were private (so maybe classes were smaller and students knew each other) and the fact that some schools played with real money rather than fake points. Years later, I revised and expanded the collection of experiments and confirmed the findings: on average, it looked like smarter groups really were more cooperative.

Of course, there *could* just be something special about being at a high-SAT school that makes people want to cooperate, something other than the cognitive skills of the students. Maybe there's a stronger campus culture at elite schools. (If so, that might be evidence that groups with higher cognitive skills tend to build more tightly knit cultures—a possibility worth exploring in its own right.) Or maybe professors at lower-scoring schools made the prisoner's dilemma experiments more difficult in some way that was difficult to measure. As I noted in the original paper, a study looking at cooperation rates across different universities could only offer a *"prima facie"* case that group test scores cause group cooperation. It would be good to know what would happen if you really ran an experiment in which you had some college students play a repeated prisoner's dilemma game and then had them take an IQ test.

That's just what I later did with the help of my colleagues Omar al-Ubaydli and Jaap Weel.[12] They're both experimental economists—the kind who spend time handing out cash to college students in order to get them to jump through carefully designed hoops. We had students show up in groups of about eight at a time for our experiment. Then we randomly paired students to play a ten-round repeated prisoner's dilemma game against each other over a computer. They never saw who they were playing against but they did know they were playing a ten-round game. However, they weren't told what game they were playing. In an experiment, you don't want to tell students, "Option 1 is 'Cooperate,' and Option 2 is 'Cheat,' which would you prefer?" That's known as "priming the subject" or "experimenter demand." Students usually want to show that they're good, moral people, so they're more likely to choose the nice response if you label it as the nice response.

So instead, we just showed them the payoffs from different actions on the screen and then gave them a choice of playing, say, "blue" or "green" rather than "cooperate" or "cheat." And how did they play? Just as you would expect on the basis of the Three Ps of the RPD: pairs with high average IQs were much more likely to cooperate—a fifteen-point rise in the pair's average IQ predicted an 11 percent rise in *both* people cooperating. Smarter pairs just found a way to make it work.

The next question is *why* are they cooperating? How do they make it work? In our ten-round game, we found that Round 2 was quite special: in that round, higher-IQ individuals apparently looked at what their opponent in Round 1 had done, and followed something like tit for tat. If their opponent cooperated, the more intelligent were more likely than the less intelligent to return the cooperation. So in Round 2, higher-IQ players were more likely to follow the norm of reciprocity; they acted like "conditional cooperators."[13] And in the world of cooperation experiments, conditional cooperators, players who are willing to play nice but only if others are playing nice, are a key ingredient in building cooperative groups.[14]

My finding with Omar and Jaap is similar to the finding from the truck-driver study. In both cases, higher-IQ players tended to be nicer, more generous, to someone who had recently treated them generously. Reciprocity is so important to explaining human behavior that economists Samuel Bowles and Herbert Gintis, who were mentioned in Chapter 1 and who both have a long history of studying human origins, sometimes refer to human beings not as *homo sapiens*—man the knower—but as *homo reciprocans*—man the reciprocator.[15] And in a variety of settings, it appears that people with higher test scores are more likely to be reciprocators.

And here's the most exciting result from my experiments with Omar and Jaap: on average, over the course of the entire experiment, higher-IQ pairs were five times more cooperative than higher-IQ individuals. The link between IQ and cooperation was an emergent phenomenon; it arose not from smart individual players but from smart pairs of players.

Recently, Aldo Rustichini and coauthors ran their own repeated prisoner's dilemma game, and it confirmed our findings.[16] Like us they gave all the players Raven's IQ tests. Unlike in our study, their game ended randomly, with an electronic flip of the coin, so players could never be sure which round was the last one. This helps keep alive the shadow of the future, the incentive to be kind because your actions today are shaping the reputation you'll have tomorrow. Rustichini's findings are right there in the title of the paper: "Higher Intelligence Groups Have Higher Cooperation Rates in the Repeated Prisoner's Dilemma." It's possible that the link between IQ and cooperation won't seem like any great surprise to you: these experiments are just games, an IQ test is a game, and people who are good at one kind of game are often good at other games. *But life is a game as well.*

Other similar experiments have been run looking at the link between IQ and game outcomes both in formal game theory experiments and in loosely structured negotiation games. In negotiation games—popular in business schools—two players pretend to work out the details of a construction deal or a product delivery schedule or some other similarly complicated and loose business deal. I discussed one such experiment in the Introduction. After the experiment is over the experimenter can check and see: Did individual students with higher SAT or GRE scores get a bigger slice of pie? Did pairs of students with higher average scores tend to grow a bigger pie altogether? It turns out that the strongest result is that *pair* test scores predict a bigger pie overall. Smarter pairs leave less money on the table on average: they find more win-win deals. There's some evidence overall that higher-scoring individual players get a bigger slice of a fixed pie, but the more interesting and more robust evidence is that higher-scoring pairs bake a bigger pie in the first place. There have been enough of these studies—both the formal prisoner's-dilemma-style games and the informal negotiation games—that one group of authors were able to perform a meta-analysis.[17] They checked to see if, taken as whole, looking across many studies, IQ-type tests were good predictors of cooperative behavior. The answer: yes, higher standardized test scores tend to predict win-win behavior.

Machiavelli and the Mind

Such cooperative tendencies [among early humans] probably evolved in two main ways. First, they are a by-product of the evolution of intelligence. As human intelligence developed, individuals could increasingly calculate that their long-term interest lay in keeping rather than breaking certain kinds of agreement. . . .
Paul Seabright, *The Company of Strangers*[18]

The positive link between IQ and cooperation is likely to be strongest in settings that involve an element of time, when there's room for social feedback. Indeed, the one study of which I'm aware that finds that higher-IQ individuals are more cruel and less cooperative is a study of a one-shot prisoner's dilemma, something much like the true criminal's prisoner's dilemma.[19] Two strangers choose exactly once, simultaneously, to either cooperate or defect: this is the only setting I know of in which high scorers are more brutal than low scorers. To my mind, this finding—that higher IQ predicts cruelty in one-shot interactions but cooperation in long-run relationships—fits with the widely discussed concept of "Machiavellian intelligence." The Machiavellian intelligence hypothesis is the theory that human intelligence exists partly to solve the most complex problem of all: the problem of living with other humans. In a one-shot environment, if it's either steal or be robbed, and if the players will never see each other again, then I'd expect higher-IQ individuals to figure out what setting they're in and act shrewdly, act cruelly. But when it's a repeated game, or even when it feels more like a repeated game with one player moving first and another player moving second, as in McCabe's trust game, I'd often expect the higher-scoring individuals to "take a chance" on trust just to see how it works out. In the field of psychology it's well-known that higher IQ predicts greater openness to new experiences, a greater willingness to try new things out.[20] In addition to being more open to new things, the person with the higher test score is more likely to understand the rules, more likely to figure out when being nice is worth it and when it's a fool's errand, and more likely to figure out when it's best to cut her losses when the investment in kindness isn't paying off. Assessing the situation: that's a skill one would expect to be more common among people with higher test scores. If an entire group of individuals with higher IQs are together for a reasonably long period of time, we should expect them to find more win-win outcomes, growing a bigger pie that they can squabble over later.

I can't tell you how many times I've met people from all walks of life who've told me that smarter people lack common sense, that they overthink and overstrategize issues to their detriment. If that were the case then smarter groups would likely turn out to be "too big for their britches" and collapse into endless rounds of cheating; failed attempts at exploitation; and continual, costly punishment. Certainly that happens sometimes, but on average, that is not the case. Now that we've seen that higher-IQ groups tend to be more cooperative, let's take that idea from the laboratory into the world of politics.

Chapter 6

PATIENCE AND COOPERATION AS INGREDIENTS FOR GOOD POLITICS

> And the main, most serious problem of social order and progress is . . . the problem of having the rules obeyed, or preventing cheating. As far as I can see there is no intellectual solution of that problem.
> **FRANK KNIGHT, "INTELLECTUAL CONFUSION ON MORALS AND ECONOMICS"**[1]

OFTEN, THE ABILITY TO STICK TO AN AGREEMENT is a matter of life and death. Robert Axelrod, in *The Evolution of Cooperation*, tells the story of French and German soldiers in World War I, buried in trenches, facing each other across the no man's land of mines and barbed wire.[2]

Each side faced a prisoner's dilemma: regardless of whether the other side was shooting or not, the best short-run option for your side was to shoot. Better to kill than to be killed, after all. The life you save may be your own, plus there was status in the form of medals and promotions for good soldiers to earn. If both sides saw it that way, then bloodshed was inevitable. However, even though simple logic said, "There will be blood," there were, nevertheless, long stretches when all was quiet on the Western front. Logic seemed to say war, but reality often said peace. Why? Axelrod said this was due to the power of tit for tat, which we discussed in Chapter 5. German soldiers and French soldiers tacitly created their own unwritten peace treaties: if you don't shoot at our side, we won't shoot at yours. And if the higher-ups *do* force us to do fire our artillery, we'll intentionally aim short of your position, or aim long of it. These rules were never written down, and they were rarely even spoken as far as we can tell—but they left their mark.

Take this example. One day the German artillery fired toward the British side without doing any damage. A German infantryman climbed up on a parapet just to deliver an apology to the British: "We are very sorry about that; we hope no one was hurt. It is not our fault, it is that damned Prussian artillery."[3] The German infantryman didn't want to destroy the fragile truce they had created with their alleged enemies. Military higher-ups hated this tacit cooperation across enemy lines. Fortunately for the officers (but not for the enlisted men) there was a simple solution: move troops around. By swapping one division south two kilometers and another north two kilometers, military officers could turn a repeated prisoner's dilemma into a literal one-shot game. Without Axelrod's "shadow of the future" looming over no man's land, war returned in earnest, and a fragile, tacit peace was destroyed.

Politics: Like War but Longer

[T]he prisoner's dilemma stands at the interface between economics and political science. ... It also augments our understanding of why governments may be inefficient. ...

Peter Ordeshook, *Game Theory and Political Theory*[4]

The story of trench warfare reminds us that the theoretical concept of the repeated prisoner's dilemma applies to real, high-stakes situations. It shows that people can create unwritten rules and can have good reasons to stick to those rules, even when there is no outside enforcer. These soldiers didn't have a government, a judiciary, or a legal system that could enforce their rules: they just had each other. Who watched these watchmen? Nobody. But all the same they were able to create and stick to rules on a fairly routine basis.

Further, this tale from the pages of history reminds us that people's beliefs about the long run have a major influence on how they act today. If you and your opponents both have long time horizons, it makes more sense to try out a peace deal. But if time is short, if one side is being moved two kilometers up the battlefield, if one side believes that tomorrow is a mere theory while today is all that exists, then the shadow of the future fades toward irrelevance and the dogs of war are more likely to slip loose again. *Carpe diem*—seize the day—is an argument for war.

If a long time horizon and pro-cooperation skills pay off on the battlefield, do they also pay off in the parliament? And if they do pay off in parliament, does that mean more prosperity for the nations ruled by cooperative parliaments? Here, I'll provide some reasons for thinking that the answer to both questions is yes. Politics, as we'll see, is full of repeated prisoner's dilemmas and other situations in which patience pays.

Consider just a few examples of prisoner's dilemmas in politics. A majority party respects unfavorable election returns even though it could declare the results invalid: the party does this partly because it knows that what goes around comes around. The president and the legislature each make compromises adding up to billions of dollars rather than fighting each other tooth and nail for each branch's favored position. Legislative committees with vague, overlapping jurisdictions respect each other's territory rather than poach a hot political issue. Branches of the military cooperate with each other on routine military missions rather than jockeying for maximum influence and maximum visibility. Yes, in the real world conflict does occur in each of these cases, but in reasonably competent bureaucracies we avoid maximum bloodshed. In other words, each case is a prisoner's dilemma in which the worst-case scenario is routinely avoided, in which a short-term benefit is regularly sacrificed because tomorrow is another day. *Carpe diem* is set aside, just as it should be.

I contend that economic institutions—property rights, legal systems, political regimes—are often a collection of just the kinds of games for which higher average IQ pays off, games that are played day in and day out by judges, bureaucrats, politicians, and citizens. If I'm right, then countries whose citizens do well on standardized tests will tend to create more secure property rights, have judges who are more honest, and create political regimes in which the key players tend to find win-win solutions to problems rather than descending into a Hobbesian war of all against all. In these countries, governments will tend to be more trustworthy. I'll provide reasons for thinking that in general, groups with higher average cognitive skills build governments that are better at creating long-term wealth. And economist Ronald Coase, whose Nobel-winning idea, the Coase Theorem, bridges the land of game theory and the land of politics, is a crucial figure in this story.

Ronald Coase and the Astonishing Power of Haggling

Informally, we can sum up the Coase Theorem this way: if it's easy for two or more parties to bargain with each other, they can bargain to an efficient, win-win outcome regardless of which party has the most power going in to the negotiation. Here's an example of the Coase theorem, perhaps the most common one. A fishery is downstream from a heavily polluting factory; to keep it simple, let's imagine no one else lives nearby. In a pro-environmentalist country, the fishery would have a right to a clean river, and therefore it could legally shut down the factory. But here's what makes it a negotiation rather than an edict: in this particular country, the fishery is legally allowed to sell the right to pollute. The factory would pay the fishery, and they'd strike a pollution-permission deal. For the right price, the fishery could let the factory poison the waters a little or a lot. But if polluting more means paying more, the factory will start to look for inexpensive ways to cut back on pollution, not out of kindness, but out of pure greed.

Consider: if the polluting factory had been making a fantastic product that people really wanted—a trendy tablet computer, perhaps—then the factory might find it profitable to pay the fishery for the right to pollute to a moderate degree. And if the fishery were motivated by self-interest, the fishery's owners would weigh the cash offer against the downside of the polluted waters and the filthier fish. Of course, if the factory is highly profitable it will also look for other, cheaper ways to achieve its goal of staying in business: in the real world, it might give outright bribes to the fishery's manager or it might engage in skullduggery, but let's set those very real options aside. For the sake of our story, what matters is that when faced with the prospect of having to pay to pollute, the factory will look into cheap ways to cut back on pollution.

So if you give the fishery the right to clean water, and if the fishery is allowed to sell part of that right to the factory, then both the fishery and the factory have an incentive to weigh the real costs of pollution and fewer fish against the real benefits of extra tablet computers. Ultimately, the two sides will come to some kind of agreement, some level of pollution, some level of fish and computers. But the Coase Theorem contains an even bigger idea: if it really is easy to bargain, you might well reach exactly the same pollution level even if the government had swapped the rights. If instead the factory had the unlimited right to pollute, then the fishery would come hat in hand to the factory owners, offering cash to the factory in exchange for cleaner river water. Your personal morality might tell you that's not the way things should be—fisheries shouldn't have to pay cash for clean water—and maybe that isn't the way things should be, but an overarching theme of Coase's work, with his theorem and in other writings, is an implicit call to dial down the moral outrage in order to get people thinking about what kinds of social systems achieve efficient, productive, fruitful outcomes. And what the Coase Theorem shows is that in some simple cases, if all sides are good at bargaining to win-win outcomes, you'll get the same amount of pollution, the same number of fish, the same number of tablet computers regardless of who owns the rights over the river. All that would differ is who paid whom: whichever party owns the river rights gets the better deal, but either way both parties weigh the benefits of more computer production against the costs of fewer fish and more river pollution.

Parliament: A Coasian Negotiation Forum

As economist Donald Wittman noted in his excellent book *The Myth of Democratic Failure*, the Coase theorem also applies to democratic legislatures.[5] In a democracy, the "property rights"—the right to make a final, binding decision—belong to the majority. So if it's easy to bargain, if both sides are good at win-win thinking, the minority should be able to bribe the majority to get to a reasonably efficient outcome. The majority proposes crippling taxes on a key profitable industry? That industry might counteroffer, suggesting an alternative, more efficient tax—perhaps a lump-sum tax based solely on past profits—that raises the same amount of money without deterring future innovation. The majority is proposing a dramatically higher minimum wage to score political points? The fast-food industry might recommend tinkering with the proposal—phasing it in, creating a lower minimum wage for younger workers—to shrink the downside. Money won't willingly be left on the table, though most of the benefits will, for better or worse, go to the majority.

Of course this all turns on the negotiation skills of both parties. If the legislative majority and the legislative minority are good at negotiating, then your nation is more likely to get the win-win outcome. But if the two factions are weaker at negotiating they're more likely to wind up with a win-lose or even a lose-lose scenario. And while Wittman applied the Coase theorem to democratic governments, the same line of reasoning applies to any government to at least some degree: autocracies and monarchies and commercial oligarchies would typically prefer to grow the pie as long as the pie eventually gets sliced in favor of the well-connected insiders.

You can start to see the power of the Coase theorem: it gives economists and other social scientists tools for analysis and for advice. It helps answer "What's going on?" and "What can we do to make this better?" It also makes inefficient outcomes stand out more starkly than ever. There's so much filth on the streets that home values are falling, you say? What keeps homeowners from lobbying local government to get better garbage collectors? What keeps homeowners from chipping in to hire someone to pick up trash once a week?

Oh, you say that homeowners can't legally compel all the neighbors to chip in? Some people want to get the benefits of a clean neighborhood without paying their share? That's a real problem—"free riding," economists call it—but perhaps one might imagine a distant future, purely hypothetical of course, in which real estate developers create housing developments with mandatory homeowners' association fees to pay for extra cleanup. You get the idea: negotiating is genuinely hard—that's one constant when it comes to the Coase theorem—but when the prize on the other side of the negotiation is large enough, all parties will be stretching for some way to grab it. People will think up new ways to turn lose-lose into win-win.

"Imposing Order on Chaos"

Men must use their own intelligence in imposing order on chaos, intelligence not in the scientific problem-solving but in the more difficult sense of finding and maintaining agreement among themselves.
James Buchanan, *The Limits of Liberty*[6]

Remember, in a one-shot prisoner's dilemma, the rational choice is not the Coasian win-win outcome. In a one-shot prisoner's dilemma, the rational thing to do is defect: cheat on your spouse, pull a gun on the cowboy at the other end of the tumbleweed-blown street, or tell your friends that, as my colleague Russ Roberts once wrote, "If you're paying, I'll have top sirloin."[7] But the efficient Coasian outcome is for everyone to give a little in order to get a better outcome. In the Coasian world we agree to be faithful, to discuss our differences like reasonable people, to order the chicken sandwich so the restaurant bill doesn't shoot sky-high. In the previous chapter, we saw one way to get that efficient outcome: repeat the game enough with patient, pleasant, and perceptive players, and you'll get quite a lot of efficiency. You'll get a lot of trustworthiness, peace, and frugality.

So suppose our fishery and factory aren't in a country with a good legal system and, as a result, the fishery can't sign a legally binding contract with the factory. But, it *can* engage in tit for tat. When the factory cuts pollution this year, the fishery makes a generous contribution to the factory CEO's favorite charity the next year. If the factory cheats and spikes up the pollutants, well, there'll be less money next year for the Friends of Leukemia Survivors. This tit-for-tat strategy can hold the factory owner's feet to the fire.

This doesn't just apply to tacit agreements between firms: it matters in politics as well. Why do powerful, popular politicians step down from office? Why don't they embezzle as much money as possible when in power? Clearly they do in some countries—so why not in all? The Coase theorem—and the theory of repeated games—provides an answer.

Confiscation and Its Cure

Routine corruption—twenty dollars to overlook a parking ticket, a thousand dollars to open a new liquor store—probably isn't the biggest threat to prosperity. While awful and degrading, it just doesn't add up to enough to shape the entire economy. It's the threat of total government confiscation of wealth, not the threat of nickel-and-dime bribery, that presents the bigger threat and the bigger intellectual conundrum. After all, the government (usually) has the most weapons, so every day the private sector is allowed to keep some wealth for itself presents a kind of puzzle. Maybe in *your* country the government is too nice to take everything for itself, but what about all those other countries?

There are, of course, quite a few countries on the planet where the government is strong enough to grab almost everything, but where nevertheless quite a lot of wealth stays in the private sector. The oil-rich countries tend to be a clear counterexample worth thinking about: the government knows where the wealth is (under the ground), so the government makes sure to own the ground and the richest people in the country are those in or very close to the government. In rich countries with large private sectors, by contrast, the government may tax quite a lot but only a moderate slice of those tax dollars is kept by top government workers: most of those tax dollars are returned to citizens as retirement checks, health care services, and education services. Top government workers and political leaders aren't poor, but in most rich countries they don't litter the "richest citizens" lists.

How do governments in rich countries resist the temptation to grab wealth? Why are some governments able to strike a Coase-style bargain with citizens, so that the private sector continues to create wealth and the government agrees to only skim off some of it? Daron Acemoglu, the leading development economist of his generation, has thought about this question a lot. He argues that governments find it difficult to make commitments to their citizens, so the world of politics always threatens to become a world of defection, of short-run behavior. But according to Acemoglu, despite their focus on the short term, governments will still sometimes find solutions to the problem of short-run temptation.[8] And once again, patience will play a key role.

Will Government Wait?

The limited time-span of decision-makers is important in relation to the capital-goods feature of law....

James Buchanan, *The Limits of Liberty*[9]

Suppose you're a businessperson trying to decide whether to invest in a long-term project. For this project, let's assume that it's obvious to you—and pretty obvious to outsiders—that the longer your project lasts, the better chance you have of striking it rich. The pie grows a little bigger every day. If you know your politicians are short-sighted and impulsive, then you'll suspect that any day could be the day they come in and grab half (or all) of your stuff. And if you know that's likely to happen in the future then you'll take that fact into account today: you'll probably never start the project in the first place for fear that your property will soon be confiscated. But if instead you know your politicians are farsighted and patient, then you'll suspect that they'll be happy taxing you slowly, taking a little slice of the pie every so often. After all, the pie is growing, so to a patient government a small slice of the pie every year for many years is worth more than 100 percent of a tiny pie today.

So if the *only* difference across countries were that some governments were more patient than others, what would we see? In the countries with impatient governments we'd see businesspeople who never took on big long-run projects and only took on smaller projects that were easy to hide from the tax authorities. At the same time, perhaps a small number of well-connected billionaires might be able to bribe tax authorities or find some other way to work around the low-quality government. An outsider might make the mistake of thinking that the businesspeople in a country like this had a "bad culture" and that they lacked "forward thinking" or "dynamism" or any of a number of pop-business catchphrases—but, really, the entrepreneurs in this country are just responding rationally to an impulsive, short-sighted government.

And what would we see in countries with patient governments? Entrepreneurs who take on big projects, small firms that occasionally grow to become medium-sized firms, and a high level of investment spending. And we'd expect to see moderate taxation on firms big and small alike. Patient governments would take a good-sized slice every year rather than pouncing on every firm that grows large enough to tax. Patient governments play the long game. This is a reminder that it's foolish to blame national economic outcomes simply on the human capital in the private sector: government impatience spurs the private sector to look for quick money, money that's easy to hide from the tax collector. Government impatience spurs the private sector to behave impatiently. And notice that all of this works without any true prisoner's dilemma: the thousands or millions of businesspeople just notice what kind of government they live under—patient or impatient—and respond accordingly.

Acemoglu explicitly recognized the major role that government impatience played in his story. The more patient the government, according to his theory, the more the private sector has reason to trust the government, and so the more the private sector invests in the future. Acemoglu even goes further, and with a bit of math creates a scenario in which if the government is patient enough, you can get a thoroughly healthy private sector and a government with a healthy level of tax revenue, all because the government behaves prudently. And all this happens because of the government's patience, not because there's some outside force such as a written constitution or international law forcing the government to behave.

Acemoglu describes this best of all practical worlds as one in which a "political Coase theorem" holds. If the government is patient enough, the government and the private sector find a way to think win-win.

Governments: Overcoming Temptation with Patience

It can be plausibly argued that much of the economic backwardness in the world can be explained by the lack of mutual confidence.
Kenneth Arrow, "Gifts and Exchanges"[10]

Most mathematical models of politics that focus on the long run include a role for patience. But political scientists and economists who create these models usually treat patience as a fixed value, something not up for debate. Acemoglu is one important exception to the rule; let's look at another.

Start with a simple, Nobel-winning example: the inflation temptation. Governments around the world would love to do two contradictory things, in the following order:

Step 1: Promise low long-term inflation, typically a popular policy.

Step 2: Once businesses set their prices at a low level, and workers start working at modest wages, print some extra money and give it to consumers; this would create a popular short-term economic boom.

One way for the country to achieve the first step would be to promise a stable supply of money. But one way to achieve the second step would be to break that promise a few months down the road. Of course, reasonable businesses and workers might well figure out the inflation temptation. So back at step one, workers insist on higher wages and businesses set their prices higher. This pair of facts—that governments want to make promises today that they will be strongly tempted to break, plus the fact that the private sector takes account of tomorrow's broken promises when making today's plans—is known as the problem of "the time inconsistency of optimal plans." Economists Finn Kydland and Ed Prescott won the Nobel Prize, in part, for showing how time inconsistency is everywhere in the world of government planning.[11] Following are a few more examples of time inconsistency in government.

> The government of Country X promises that foreign investors will be treated fairly, because Country X wants lots of foreign direct investment. But foreigners know that their investments will be confiscated down the road, regardless of the verbal or legal promises: the foreigners are aware of the confiscation temptation. Therefore, the foreigners invest very little, or, like Francisco d'Anconia in *Atlas Shrugged*, they only use old, outdated, decrepit equipment in their overseas operations—equipment that will be of little use to the government of Country X when it predictably confiscates the equipment.

Country Y promises a transparent legal system that will be fair to businesses owned by ethnic minorities. But ethnic minorities know that they aren't a big enough group to sway an election, so the government of Country Y won't keep its promise. As a result, the minority groups don't build large businesses, and instead work as employees or in the underground economy. And so the entire economy ends up poorer, since society never really makes use of the skills of its ethnic minorities.

The government in Country Z promises never to give disaster aid to people who live in flood zones to try to keep people from moving there. But people know that the government can't resist the temptation to give disaster aid after a flood so people go right on building homes in flood zones. When disaster comes the checks are cut a few weeks after the floods—and so the people's beliefs are vindicated (This example is actually from Kydland and Prescott's original article).

A government in an unnamed country passes a law promising never to bail out big banks if a financial crisis ever happens, but . . . actually, you can probably write the rest of this example yourself.

These are just a few examples of how a government *wishes* it could keep its promises, but just can't find a way to do it—the temptation to cheat is just too strong. Governments find it difficult to tie their own hands. But once again, the power of patience will come to the rescue: once again, groups that are more patient will be more likely to reap the rewards of a better economy, while the less patient will be stuck in the one-shot world of suboptimal plans. Patience can make the optimal plan into a time consistent plan.

Economists Robert Barro and Robert Gordon were early to point this out. If you take Kydland and Prescott's simple two-period story and lengthen it out to an endless number of periods, then you find yourself in a world in which reputation matters.[12]

And fortunately, that theoretical world is exactly like the real world: just as your grandmother taught you, a good reputation is worth many rubies. And Barro and Gordon note that patience is crucial to getting that reputation. People who focus on the long run care more about their reputations.

In a world in which reputation matters, citizens can "punish" a government that breaks its promises by simply not believing the government for a while. So if the government dramatically raises business taxes after promising to keep them low, investors can "punish" the government through the common-sense response of not trusting the government for a decade or so. In practice, this means that investors avoid new investments, hide more investments in the underground economy or in tax shelters, or invest overseas in more trustworthy countries. So the government—and the private economy—really suffer. And when the government gets its act together and tries again to promise a "business friendly" tax regime, citizens will be fearful at first, but if time goes by without a tax spike, citizens will start trusting again and investing more in the taxable sectors of the economy. So what will tempt the government to cheat and spike up taxes, print more money, confiscate foreign investment, or exploit ethnic minorities? Impatience. When the shadow of the future is distant and hazy, the prospects for lower inflation, fairer treatment of minority groups, and pro-investment policies fade into the ether.

Test Scores and Government Quality: Theory Against the Facts

The prisoner's dilemma experiments, the negotiation games, and tests of patience all show links between IQ and good outcomes in lab experiments, and all three are part of mainstream models of why good government is so very hard to come by. The links in the chain are there, but do the links hold together in the real world?

Do nations with higher average test scores have less corruption, better governance, more trustworthy political systems?

Overall, yes. The Corruption Perceptions Index—a widely used measure of honest, transparent government—correlates strongly with national average IQ, as Figure 6.1 shows. And Niklas Potrafke of the Munich research institute IFO has found that national test scores predict national corruption even when you take account of the fact that high-average-IQ countries tend to be richer, have better educated citizens, and have many other features going for them.[13] Average IQ predicts lower corruption across countries. Additional research that Potrafke and I collaborated on showed that both national average IQ and national math and science test scores do a robust job of predicting a nation's degree of overall property rights enforcement.[14] And University of Johannesburg

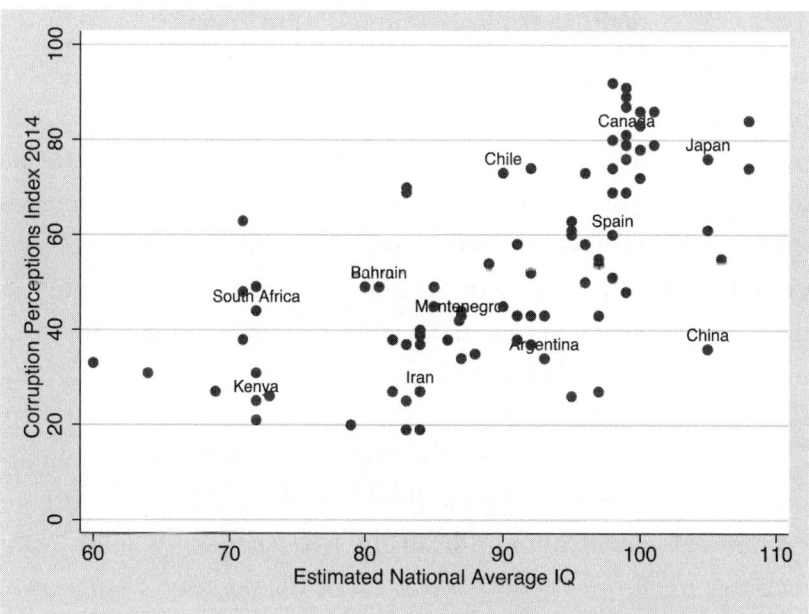

FIGURE 6.1 Estimated national average IQ and 2014 Corruption Perceptions Index.
Source: Lynn and Meisenberg, "National IQs Calculated" and 2014 Corruption Perceptions Index.

economist Isaac Kalonda Kanyama found a moderate to strong relationship between national average IQ and yet another set of institutional quality indices created by the World Bank.[15] In nations with higher average test scores, politicians tend to respect people's property, government bureaucracies allow people and businesses to buy and sell with less interference, and bribery is less a part of daily life. In nations with higher average test scores, the government is more likely to let people and businesses find their Coasian bargains peacefully. In these settings, it appears that Machiavellian intelligence often becomes Coasian intelligence. The relationship between test scores and government quality is strong enough that it should be part of any serious discussion about how to improve governance. Human capital, proxied by national test scores, appears to be an important ingredient for creating good governance.

Where Do Politicians Come From?

But let's turn to an important question: Why should the average IQ of government officials have anything to do with the average IQ of the nation's citizens? The most important reason is that governments are almost always run by people from the country being governed, and ordinary probability theory gives us good reasons to think that even if politicians tend to be far above average in their country (a debatable proposition), politicians in higher-scoring countries are likely to have more skills than politicians in lower-scoring countries. Of course, not all countries are governed by politicians from their own country: many countries have been colonized. But most countries today are run by domestic residents, so whether politicians are routinely drawn at random from the population or whether they tend to come from the top 10 percent of the population, there will be a general tendency for countries with high average test scores to have leaders with high average test scores. Rindermann and his coauthors found that nations with higher average test scores tend to be led by politicians with more formal education; the correlation was modest, but, more important, it was in the right direction.[16] And since education helps predict IQ, the theory that countries with higher national test scores usually have higher-scoring politicians has some evidence in its favor.

To get the opposite result—to get above-average-IQ countries with below-average-IQ leaders—you'd need to have systematically lower standards for politicians in high-IQ countries. Perhaps that's plausible to you, perhaps not. Those of us in rich countries enjoy mocking the intelligence of our politicians, but every U.S. president after Reagan has held a degree from an Ivy League institution—institutions that, joking aside, are not famous for letting in people with below-average test scores. And that's just one example: the bureaucracies of the developed countries have a reputation for, if anything, being overweighted, not underweighted, with people from the most elite schools, schools that screen for admission with IQ-type tests. On average, politicians will tend to have higher average test scores when their nations have higher average test scores. That means that raising national average IQ through nutritional and medical improvements could well provide long-run political payoffs. One can only hope.

Chapter 7

INFORMED VOTERS AND THE QUESTION OF EPISTOCRACY

> An irrational voter does not hurt only himself. He also hurts everyone who is, as a result of his irrationality, more likely to live under misguided policies.
> **BRYAN CAPLAN, *MYTH OF THE RATIONAL VOTER*** [1]

ONE OF THE BEST INSIGHTS FROM TOXICOLOGY IS THAT "the danger is in the dosage." A small amount of poison, of toxic pesticide, of radiation, isn't as dangerous as a big dosage. Whether it's exposure to solar radiation or lead or Agent Orange, more is worse than less, and less is worse than none. Regular people tend to reject that idea: their intuition is that a little is basically as bad for you as a lot, that poison is bad, full stop. Experts disagree with the general public.

There's real evidence for this disagreement: Health researcher Nancy Kraus and coauthors surveyed toxicologists who worked for government, the private sector, and academia, and they also surveyed regular Americans, asking each group whether they agreed with claims such as "It can never be too expensive to reduce the risks associated with chemicals," "Use of chemicals has improved our health more than it has harmed it," and "It's not how much of the chemical that you are exposed to that should worry you, but whether or not you are exposed at all."[2] You might think that toxicologists who were professors or government workers might be especially opposed to artificial chemicals—after all, if they say that "chemicals are pretty safe overall" they might be talking themselves out of a job—but it turns out that the differences in opinion between different kinds of toxicologists were pretty small compared to the differences between toxicologists and the general public. In the survey, only 12 percent of the general public strongly agreed with the claim that the danger is in the dosage, while 62 percent of toxicologists strongly agreed with the same claim. Notice the massive gap: a difference of 50 percentage points between experts and the general public. A similar pattern showed up in other questions: the general public tends to see the danger of chemicals as a great opportunity to apply all-or-nothing reasoning, while the experts tend to see toxicity as a matter of degree.

So what predicts whether people agree with toxicologists? Education: people with more education are more likely to agree with the experts, more likely to agree with peer-reviewed science, more likely to think that being poisoned is a matter of degree. People with more education tend to know more facts.

This matters in a democracy. If voters have better information, they are more likely to form their political opinions on the basis of reality rather than rumor, intuition, and wishful—or fearful—thinking. Social scientists have tested this claim in a variety of ways in recent decades. For instance, in one study, American, British, and Finnish citizens were all more likely to correctly answer serious news questions about politics, science, and the economy if they had more education; of the four countries in the study, Denmark was the only nation where education levels didn't predict news knowledge.[3] Americans with more education were substantially more likely to know economic facts such as how large the deficit was in the year they were surveyed, more likely to know that most Americans pay more in payroll (Social Security and Medicare) taxes than in income taxes, and more likely to know other basic facts about economic policy.[4] Educated voters have more political knowledge as well. They're more likely to know the name of their member of Congress, how many years a senator serves, how many members there are on the Supreme Court. Those facts might just be mere trivia, but even if they are, then recall the power of the da Vinci Effect: people who do well on trivia tests tend to do well on the other parts of an IQ test as well. Skills predict skills.

How much do informed voters matter in a democracy? My colleague Bryan Caplan has written probably the best-known research on the question, which he pulls together in his surprisingly entertaining book *The Myth of the Rational Voter*, a book that deeply informs everything I say in this chapter. Caplan argues that a major failing of modern democracies is that they do a pretty good job of responding to the outlandish preferences of voters. Politicians who don't give the voters what they want might be replaced by those who will—politics is a reasonably competitive sport—so the will of the average voter matters. But voters have little incentive to become informed about whether their policy views are correct— about whether a higher minimum wage will destroy too many jobs, about whether a boost in government spending will pay for itself by boosting private spending and tax revenues, about whether getting more students in college will grow wages or just mean more diplomas hanging on more walls. When it comes to forming political opinions, it's rational to stay uninformed.

After all, for an individual voter, whose solitary vote essentially never decides an election, the outcome of the election will be the same whether she learns a lot about the topic or not, so she has little incentive to learn about which policies have which outcomes. She knows to put gasoline, not corn syrup, in her car tank, because if she gets that decision wrong her car won't run. But if she holds the view that tax cuts grow the economy so much that tax cuts pay for themselves, and she votes accordingly, government policy won't change at all. Irrational political beliefs are free, consequenceless, and economic theory predicts that people will buy a lot of stuff that's free.

But Caplan does more than just show that "in theory" voters might be poorly informed. He shows that when it comes to economic policy, Americans disagree dramatically with professional economists about which economic policies are a good idea, which are a bad idea, and what consequences different economic reforms would have. Caplan treats economists the same way that Kraus treated toxicologists: as the experts who probably know more than the layperson. One might recall the old line about how if all the economists in the world were laid end to end, they couldn't reach a conclusion, but there's a surprising amount of agreement in our field on the basics of supply and demand, about the importance of unintended consequences, and about the power of social side effects.

In his book, Caplan showed that when economics professors and the general public were asked precisely the same questions about economic policy, there was often massive disagreement. But Caplan went further than just noting that the public disagrees with the experts. He asked, "What makes people think like economists?" One important factor? Education: the better educated you are, the more likely you are to agree with economists on the benefits of freer trade across countries, on the benefits of corporate downsizing, and on many other issues. And Caplan shows that this isn't just because economists and the well-educated are more affluent—it's not just prosperity making people callous to the needs of the less well-off. Caplan statistically controls for income and many other factors, creating a roughly apples-to-apples comparison between economists and non-economists with the same level of income, the same political party, and so on, and controlling for quite a few other personal characteristics. He finds that the overwhelming reason economists disagree with the average American is because they are economists, not because they're mostly affluent, well-educated men. And in case you were wondering, the disagreement isn't caused by economists being Republicans: economics professors are much more likely to be Democrats than Republicans.

So if education makes people think like economists, that might help explain why national average IQ predicts good economic performance across countries. Countries with high average test scores tend to have high education levels, which means that on average the high-scoring countries will have better-informed voters. In democracies, that means those politicians are going to respond to the more market-oriented beliefs of their voters by pushing through the market-oriented policies that will get them reelection. And in both nondemocracies and democracies alike, it means that a better-educated, higher-scoring population will tend to fill out the ranks of the government bureaucracy, carrying their somewhat better knowledge about economics (and toxicology) into the halls of government. We've been told all our lives that informed voters matter, and that claim is right according to Caplan.

But of course when Caplan reports that years of education predict (somewhat stronger) pro-market attitudes, one wonders whether it's the education itself that is causing the change in opinion or whether it's IQ or some other trait that just correlates with education. In later work with Stephen Miller, Caplan looks into the IQ-versus-education question.[5] They used the long-standing General Social Survey (available for free online) to see which better predicts pro-market attitudes, a person's years of education or a person's score on a simple vocabulary test. Since a vocabulary test is a component of the Wechsler IQ test, and since vocabulary skill correlates strongly with overall IQ, the vocabulary test is a reasonably good stand-in for a complete IQ test. Caplan and Miller then ran a contest: Which was the better predictor of pro-market attitudes in the General Social Survey, IQ or years of education? Overall, IQ was the winner, though not by a large margin. When it came to freer international trade, education did a better job predicting pro-market attitudes, for instance, so perhaps modern American schooling really does make you friendlier toward people in other countries or perhaps education helps people understand the Victorian-era economist David Ricardo's unintuitive "law of comparative advantage," the bedrock idea underlying the argument for free trade. But in general, IQ was a good predictor of pro-market attitudes, winning the IQ versus education race. Higher cognitive skills apparently help people think more like economists. And if economists genuinely have more information about the economy than the average person—I'll leave that for you to decide—then higher cognitive skills mean better informed voters.

Numeracy and the Informed Voter

Yale's Dan Kahan and his coauthors gave people two kinds of tables to read. One group saw a table providing data about gun violence, and another group saw data on skin rashes.[6] The researchers asked respondents whether the data in the table backed the theories that (in the first case) gun control laws reduce violence and (in the second case) a particular cream helped cure the rash.

Here's the trick: the data were all made up. As part of the experiment, Kahan asked people what political party they belonged to and how partisan they were. Also, there were two sets of gun data given out randomly to different participants, one of which made it look like gun control cut crime rates while the other made it look like gun control raised crime rates; they did the same scrambling with the rash data. The test subjects also took a short IQ-type test, a test of numerical skill. What did Kahan and coauthors find? Perhaps naturally, they found that Democrats were more likely to say the gun data supported gun control *regardless of which data they were given* and Republicans fell victim to the opposite bias. Even when the objective facts are in front of your face, even when you're asked to interpret the results of just one simple study, you're likely to see things your way. As the saying goes, where you stand depends on where you sit. But Kahan's study went further. He checked to see whether people who did well on the IQ-type test were more likely to get at the truth in both the skin rash case *and* the gun control case. And, no surprise, people who were better at math were usually more likely to get to the truth.

That's not the end of the story, though. In his inaugural essay for the news website *Vox*, journalist Ezra Klein drew out one particular finding of the Kahan study: in the gun control case, greater numeracy predicted greater disagreement between Democrats and Republicans.[7] So if the data said that gun control worked, high-scoring Republicans were only a little more likely than low-scoring Republicans to read the table correctly, but high-scoring Democrats were much more likely than low-scoring Democrats to realize that the news favored their team. Klein's lesson: the well-informed disagree more than the poorly informed. More math skill means more knowledge, and more knowledge might mean more disagreement, not more harmony.

And yes, that's one lesson to draw from Kahan's study. But here's another lesson that's equally valid: overall, people with higher IQ-type scores were more likely to read the graph correctly, even when it was news they didn't want to see. High-scoring Republicans exposed to pro-gun-control evidence were a bit more likely to interpret the data correctly than their lower-scoring fellow Republicans, while high-scoring Democrats exposed to anti-gun-control evidence were essentially unchanged in their interpretation compared to lower-scoring Democrats. And when it was news they wanted to see, the high scorers in both parties were likely to get the right answer. So overall, people with higher IQ-type scores were more likely to get to the objective truth in studies at Yale, and perhaps they get closer to the objective truth in the real world as well. Yes, you're more likely to see the light if it's light you want to see. But you're also more likely to see the light if you do better on a cognitive skill test.

The Attitudes of the Intelligent

People with higher test scores tend to hold more pro-market attitudes and are more likely to see their way through a mass of complicated, ambiguous facts to the core insight. But are they more likely to actually vote? Are they more likely to actually influence policy by showing up on election day? Or instead are they more likely to come to the insight of economist Gordon Tullock, who stopped voting once he learned that he was more likely to die in an accident on the way to the voting booth than he was to change the outcome of the election? Early studies of who votes looked at years of education, which of course has a moderate to strong relationship with IQ. In a classic study from the 1970s, aptly titled *Who Votes*, political scientists Wolfinger and Rosenstone concluded,

> The core finding is the transcendent importance of education. . . . [T]he personal qualities that raise the probability of voting are the skills that make learning about politics easier and more gratifying and reduce the difficulties of voting.[8]

The positive link between education and voting turns up in many countries. But even though IQ predicts education, and education predicts voting, we can't definitively conclude that IQ predicts voting. Even though A predicts B and B predicts C, it's still possible that A doesn't help predict C at all. So whenever possible it's good to check to see if IQ and other test scores really do predict the outcomes we care about. Showing that education predicts an outcome isn't the same as showing that IQ predicts the outcome.

So far, two studies in the United Kingdom find that higher-scoring individuals are more likely to vote, regardless of other things known about the person, such as his social class, his education, and some personality traits; one of the studies finds that higher IQ predicts a greater interest in politics as well.[9] However, a study in the United States drawing on three different surveys finds no substantial evidence that IQ predicts voting behavior. The author concludes that "[cognitive] ability's dominance in determining civic participation is empirically untenable."[10]

But the relationship between IQ and some key politically relevant attitudes is clearer: a U.K. study finds that people who do better on IQ tests are more likely to be socially liberal, less likely to hold racist attitudes, and more likely to favor gender equality.[11] So the U.K. results suggest that higher-scoring individuals are more likely to be social liberals, while the U.S. results of Caplan and Miller suggest that higher-scoring individuals are more likely to be Adam Smith–style market liberals. And in a review of some recent studies, psychologists Rindermann, Flores-Mendoza, and Woodley conclude,

> [H]igher intelligence leads to more rational worldviews, less intense religiosity, less stereotyped thinking and less dogmatism.[12]

With data from Brazil, the same authors find that people who did better on the Raven's IQ test were overall more likely to hold center or center-right political attitudes, even after differences in income, education, and other factors were taken into account. Therefore, in Brazil at least, higher-IQ individuals were more likely to avoid extremes of both left and right. Without studies from other countries one should be cautious in making generalizations, but the theory that IQ predicts a general tendency toward liberalism—in the traditional sense of the Enlightenment, a cautious blend of social tolerance and market orientation—looks like a reasonable starting point.

Informed Voters in the Real World

Cognitive skills may do more than just predict specific political attitudes: since IQ predicts memory—short run and longer term—people with higher test scores are more likely to know more facts about more topics, including about current events. And information helps to create informed voters. Along these lines, Rohini Pande of Harvard's Kennedy School took the time to review all the major studies—including real field experiments run across the developing world—that addressed a precise question: she wanted to see if giving information to voters would improve government quality.[13] You can probably guess the answer she came to—in good academic style, it was a "Yes" with caveats—but just as important as her review of the studies is her discussion of why informed voters matter. She emphasizes one key channel, quite different from the more ideological channels that Caplan discusses. Pande argues that informed voters can hold politicians accountable: they remember if the politician was corrupt, effective, scandalous, whatever. Recalling the famous Dali painting with the melting clock—the one on the cover of Barro and Sala-i-Martin's textbook—let's call this the "persistence of memory" channel.[14] As one piece of evidence she discusses a classic study by economists Ferraz and Finan of Brazilian government audits: Brazil's central government mandated audits in some regions but not others, and so Ferraz and Finan could compare how voters treated incumbent mayors both pre- and post-audit, as well as between audited and non-audited regions.[15] Yes, the audits mattered, but it also turns out that radio mattered: radio, that key source of low-cost information for so many people around the world. In regions with more radio stations, news about local corruption hurt incumbents and news about a lack of corruption helped incumbents. The effect of audits was muted—literally—in regions without radio stations. When information about government quality is easily accessible, voters do a better job of rewarding the effective and punishing the ineffective. Toward the end of her review, Pande concludes,

> Voters in low-income settings are receptive to new information about politician performance and are willing to vote on the basis of this information.[16]

So if voters could only get more accurate information about which politicians are genuinely better and which are genuinely worse, government quality would improve. But while the transmission channel of radio is important, another kind of information transmission channel may also be important: voter memory. Voters who remember more actual facts about politicians—what they read in the paper or heard on TV a month ago—are better able to discipline badly performing politicians. Voting is partly a trivia test (who's that person running for mayor again?), and people with higher IQ scores tend to do better on trivia tests. On average, one would expect people who are good at trivia tests to do more to keep politicians accountable. This, as elsewhere, is an opportunity for future research.

The Social Construction of Opinion

Exactly what is the effect of the opinions of others on our own?
Solomon Asch, "Opinions and Social Pressure"[17]

We've seen evidence of conformity in the classroom and after a neighbor wins the lottery, but the most famous conformity study deserves a moment of our time. The classic study: social psychologist Solomon Asch puts a group of students in a room, and they're all shown three lines drawn on a piece of cardboard, labeled A, B, C. The second line is clearly the longest and C is clearly the shortest. Students are asked, one by one, to say out loud which of the lines is longest. And student after student says A. When it comes to your turn, what do you answer when everyone—or almost everyone—gives what appears to be the incorrect answer? In Asch's original study, about a third of the students give the wrong answer, A, conforming with the group.[18]

Of course, everybody in the room except for you is a trained confederate, and they're faking the answer to see if you'll conform. The Asch experiment is the classic study of human conformity, a benchmark that all other studies of conformity are compared against. And it's a sign that when much of the group tends to get the same answer, there's a multiplier effect that pushes some of the fence-sitters in the direction of the rest of the group. When Asch wrote up his experimental results for *Scientific American* back in the

1950s, the title of the article was actually "Opinions and Social Pressure." And just imagine: if a sizable number of people are willing to conform by giving an obviously wrong answer to a question about line lengths, just ask yourself how much they might conform if asked a more ambiguous question, such as whether the "danger is in the dose" or whether international trade is good for the nation.

If the Asch channel is intense enough, people who hold divergent opinions will decide to keep quiet just to avoid offending the majority, so nobody hears those divergent opinions at all, thus ensuring the demise of the offending ideas: this is political scientist Elisabeth Noelle-Neumann's *spiral of silence*.[19] Noelle-Neumann's now-classic theory has been tested repeatedly, and there's at least some evidence that the spiral is real. Once an idea is labeled as odd or outside the mainstream, some people just stop talking about it. And since there's evidence for this extreme example of idea conformity, it's likely that milder forms of idea conformity are occurring fairly often in officially free and open societies on just about every political, social, and economic topic.

But the full-blown spiral of science isn't the usual case. Usually political opinions don't spread by shutting down the competition; instead they are more likely to spread from friend to friend. For decades political scientists have studied how political opinions spread. Political scientist David Nickerson sums up the mid-twentieth-century research which found that "information flowed horizontally through networks," a finding that "overturned the opinion leadership model of media effects."[20] So from the 1950s onward, political scientists have suspected that we mostly get our political information from our peers, not from high-status elites such as political leaders, CEOs, and religious leaders. Humans are often conformers, but we look to the left and right more than we look up.

However, just because you get information from your neighbor doesn't mean your neighbor is substantially influencing your overall political worldview. After all, you might only talk to neighbors you already tend to agree with on politics. You trust your friend's politics because you largely agree with your friend already. The only real way to check to see if one person can substantially influence your politics is to randomly change the people you talk to about politics—or to randomly change what people talk to you about. Once again, experiments are the gold standard.

Of course the Asch experiment is one example, but what happens when people run Asch-type experiments on political questions? What happens when somebody has to talk about a controversial political topic in a room of conservatives versus in a room of progressives versus in a politically diverse room? A team of Yale and Notre Dame political scientists ran a series of "deliberative polling" studies to investigate these questions. They started by surveying participants' political attitudes before they were put into a room with other participants.[21] Once they were put into the room the participants were asked to discuss a prescribed set of topics such as education policy, health care policy, or the then-ongoing war in Iraq. After the discussion they were surveyed again. Participants were randomly put into different rooms, so some wound up in rooms with more Iraq war supporters, some with more war opponents, and so on. That made it possible to check whether their post-discussion opinion moved toward the pre-discussion opinion of the average person in their room: it was possible to see whether they were conforming. In total, the researchers ran 330 groups of about ten people each, so if conformity was even a modestly strong force, it should have shown up. Here's what they conclude:

> After several years of experimentation, we have found little evidence that group composition influences postdiscussion attitudes. This persistent finding, which holds across a range of experimental variations and for subgroups defined by political knowledge, suggests that the expectations of the Asch literature do not apply to the Deliberative Poll setting.[22]

So there's "little evidence" for strong conformity effects after a few hours of talking about a political topic, and since the arrangement is quite a bit like the Asch experiment—small group of strangers, some conversation, a chance to state your opinion—I take this as evidence that political opinions really are harder to budge. Other studies have found larger conformity effects—one a study of jury awards, another an earlier British study much like this Yale-Notre Dame study—but overall it appears that at least in the short run, conformity effects are fairly weak when it comes to political opinions.

That said, in politics as in medicine, it's hard to run long-term experimental studies. We'll probably never run decade-long studies that randomly assign well-informed people to some neighborhoods and less-informed people to other neighborhoods, so we probably won't get real experimental evidence of the long-run effect of conformity effects on public opinion. One could imagine such studies—when a railroad station or military base is built in one town but not another, do the new residents influence the voting patterns of the old residents?—but to my knowledge they haven't been run.

The closest example I know of is a study of Google employees. Bo Cowgill of Google worked with economists Justin Wolfers and Eric Zitzewitz to study Google's internal prediction markets, an online market in which Google employees can bet on questions such as "How many users will Gmail have" a few months in the future, what Google Talk's quality rating will be, and whether Google will open an office in Russia.[23] These markets work like sports betting markets, so players have a real incentive to guess correctly: the closer their guess is to the truth, the more they can win. Googlers don't bet for real money, but they can win prizes if they do well in the prediction markets, so the incentives to try hard are reasonably strong. As my colleague Robin Hanson notes, these internal prediction markets do a good job guessing real corporate outcomes—and are even better than the guesses of company managers: when money and prizes are on the line, passions and egos lose out, and the truth tends to bubble up. So what shapes the way people bet in these prediction markets? Cowgill's study found that the best predictor of how any individual Googler bet in the market was whom he or she sat closest to:

> [O]pinions on specific topics are correlated among employees who are proximate in some sense. Physical proximity was the most important of the forms of proximity we studied . . . [C]orrelations declined with distance for employees on the same floor of a building . . . [E]mployees on different floors of the same building were no more correlated than employees in different cities. Google employees moved offices extremely frequently during our sample period (in the US, approximately once every 90 days), and we are able to use these office moves to show that our results are not simply the result of like-minded individuals being seated together.[24]

So in a case in which there's some kind of prize on the line we see real evidence of idea conformity. Proximity drives how you behave in the Google betting market, and it appears to be at least partly because proximity drives information flow: it's easy to engage in small talk about how the Gchat bug fixes are going with somebody through the cubicle wall. At Google and in the rest of the world, it's probably a good idea to be sitting next to somebody well informed.

Short-run public opinion experiments find little evidence for idea conformity, while weeks-long betting studies at Google find a bit more evidence. I suspect that idea conformity is stronger in the long run than in the short run, that if someone randomly acquires some high-IQ or Democratic or anti-war neighbors the average person is likely to shift her opinions slightly in her neighbors' direction over the years (just as they'll drift slightly her way), but that's a conclusion I base on the repeated finding of conformity in so many other areas, not on any firm experimental evidence. When you find a sociological tendency in so many parts of life, it's reasonable to believe that the same tendency—moderate conformity—is probably going on in this part of life as well. The short-run experiments may say that peers don't matter for public opinion, but if there's ever an election in which the key issue is which line drawn on a sheet of paper is longest, we can be sure that the Asch effect will drive the election.

On Epistocracy

If a nation expects to be ignorant and free, in a state of civilization, it expects what never was and never will be.
Thomas Jefferson, 1816[25]

Jennifer Hochschild is a professor of government and of African and African-American studies at Harvard. In a provocative article, she states,

> [D]emocracies thrive best . . . if citizens have a broad education and some level of political knowledge. Education is associated with tolerance, support for rights, civic engagement; political knowledge is important for prospective voting and preferable for retrospective voting. These are empirical claims with strong historical backing. But the paradox that democratization involves extending the franchise to those least cognitively prepared to be good democratic citizens has a normative as well as empirical edge.[26]

Hochschild wrestles with the "normative edge" and concludes "[T]here are indeed costs to continually expanding the franchise to bring in those least cognitively prepared to participate in a democratic polity—but the benefits of democratization outweigh those costs."[27] Not all scholars have come to the same normative conclusion on the merits of expanding the right to vote. In the field of political philosophy the topic of "epistocracy"—rule by the informed—has resurged in the past few years. Philosopher Jason Brennan of Georgetown is one leader in the field, arguing not only that poorly informed voters should refrain from voting, but also that the poorly informed should actually be barred from voting.[28] Brennan argues that citizens of a democracy—well educated and poorly educated alike—have a right to be governed by people who are good at governing. And as surveys of voter knowledge repeatedly demonstrate, some voters are substantially more informed than others. If people genuinely do have the right to be ruled by reasonably well-informed individuals, then there may be a trade-off between two human rights: the universal right to vote and the universal right to be governed by informed citizens.

To close, here is another Jefferson quote, this from a letter to George Washington and written on the walls of the Library of Congress:

> [O]ur liberty can never be safe but in the hands of the people themselves, and that too of the people with a certain degree of instruction.

For now, let's leave the moral debates to the philosophers. As an economist I will make this forecast: if a nation can find an effective way to raise the information level of its voters, it will probably become more market-oriented, more socially tolerant, and more prosperous in the long run.

Chapter 8

THE O-RING THEORY OF TEAMS

IN 1986, THE SPACE SHUTTLE *CHALLENGER* EXPLODED shortly after take-off, killing all seven astronauts aboard. The cause of the explosion was the failure of one of the rubber O-rings—essentially rubber bands—that helped to seal the joints in the shuttle's booster rockets. The O-rings served as gasket seals, like washers in a faucet, there to ensure that burning fuel didn't leak out. It was too cold the morning of the launch, so the rubber O-rings became too rigid to maintain the seal and the burning rocket fuel escaped, heating the shuttle's massive external fuel tank and creating the fatal explosion. The failure of one O-ring was enough to cost the lives of all seven astronauts. Humans search for deep meaning in the deaths of others but often enough in war, in hospitals, and in pandemics it is the smallest of failures that can cause the greatest of losses.

Harvard economist Michael Kremer saw the O-ring story as a tale of tragedy, but he saw something else as well: he saw a parable that might help explain why workers in some countries are so much more productive than quite similar workers in other countries.[1] Kremer's O-ring theory *assumed* that some kinds of projects are like the space shuttle—in which any one failure can lead to disaster—

but after starting with that assumption he *proved* that an "O-ring economy" would look quite a lot like the world we live in. Kremer's theory can help explain why the janitors and executive assistants at top law firms earn more than people with the same jobs at ordinary law firms, why small differences in the average skill of workers across countries can cause massive differences in productivity across countries, and why the richest countries tend to produce entirely different goods than the poorest countries.

Consider a company making vases. It takes two people to make a vase, one to blow it from molten glass and a second to pack it safely for delivery. If either worker drops the vase, it's worthless and the effort was wasted. So if each worker has a 1 percent chance of dropping the vase, there's about a 98 percent chance of things going well. However, if each worker has a 50 percent chance of dropping the vase, there's only a 25 percent chance of things going well. Clearly, the owner will want workers who are good at handling vases—at least as long as safer workers aren't too much more expensive than riskier workers.

Kremer notes that a lot of the modern economy works like this vase company: computer chips with tiny errors are worthless and get thrown out; clothes with small mistakes in stitching get sent to discount stores and sell for a fraction of full price. In an O-ring economy, the clichés are true: a chain is only as strong as its weakest link; for want of a nail a battle can be lost. But Kremer goes beyond these obvious points to draw some surprising conclusions. Perhaps the most important one is that business owners will naturally—by an invisible hand—put highly skilled workers together on the most valuable projects and put lower-skilled workers together on the less valuable projects. The lower-skilled workers will earn lower wages, since they are less productive, but they won't be just a little less productive: they'll be a *lot* less productive. And we can go even further: even if the economy were run by a benevolent dictator, one who just wanted to make everyone as productive as possible, she would do the same thing, sorting workers with more skill together in one firm and sorting workers with less skill together in another firm.

Here's an example from the vase economy: suppose there are two types of workers, and two of each type of worker. Type Hi never drops a vase, and Type Lo drops a vase half the time (I'd be Type Lo for sure, at least the first day). That's four workers total, two teams of two workers each. If the benevolent dictator put the workers onto two teams, each with one Hi and one Lo worker working together, then each team would have a 50 percent success rate: the Hi team member would never drop a vase, but the Lo member would drop half of them.

If instead the Hi workers are put together on one team and the Lo workers are on another, what would happen? You'd get 100 percent perfect performance from the Hi team but 25 percent success from the Lo team. The Lo team's performance sounds just awful, but that's not the point of this story: the point is that once we switched to putting Hi workers on one team and Lo workers on another, the *average* success rate per team rose from 50 percent beforehand to 62.5 percent (the average of 100 percent and 25 percent). The benevolent dictator, in her quest to produce the most vases possible, ends up doing the same thing that a profit-centered capitalist would do: she puts the more-skilled workers onto one team and the less-skilled workers onto another team. With a bigger pie there's now more to share.

An economic theorist could summarize Kremer's result with this mouthful:

> Strategic complementarities in production lead to endogenous sorting by worker skill.

But since Kremer's work, economists have tended to sum up cases like this by saying, "That's a fragile O-ring technology" or "Clearly, that's an O-ring sector of the economy: since one mistake can destroy most of the value, companies will either be obsessed with perfection or they just won't try that hard at all."

Here is one modern example of an O-ring production method that we're all familiar with: moviemaking. Why do award-winning directors team up with award-winning cinematographers and get a musical score by elite composers such as Ennio Morricone or John Williams or Hans Zimmer? Why do the best tend to work with the best—and the not-quite-best with the not-quite-best? Perhaps it's all just ego, but at least some of the time it's surely the production company—the people with financial skin in the game—insisting that the famous director team up with the famous cinematographer rather than the famous director's buddy from film school. At the lower end of the profession, producers don't think to themselves, "Well, this movie is probably going to go direct to basic cable, but if I could just get a top composer or if I could get Industrial Light and Magic to do the effects, that'd make it a solid $200 million blockbuster." Of course the direct-to-cable producer would love to get John Williams if he were cheap enough, but there's no way a normal John Williams wage will yield a John Williams return on a clunker of a movie. Even if a *Raiders*-quality score were guaranteed to double revenues, two times $1 million is just $2 million, and that probably won't be enough to pay the John Williams wage.

There's a bigger lesson behind these tales of vases and movies: O-ring thinking gets us away from addition and pushes us toward exponents—when doubling a small number still yields a pretty small number, but doubling *two* small numbers—and then multiplying them together—can yield a huge number. It's not that a bad musical score completely ruins a great movie, but if a weak score had cut *Avatar*'s sales by just 2 percent, then James Cameron would've lost over $20 million in ticket sales. Scrimping on a tunesmith is, as Ben Franklin would say, penny wise but pound foolish.

O-ring technologies produce products that are delicate, fragile, and easy to break. Of course the products don't have to be actual physical products. The lawyers working on a billion-dollar corporate merger are probably working with an O-ring technology, in which one typo can mean a $100 million lawsuit down the road, and if you're having open heart surgery it's probably a good idea to have the best nurses, the best cardiologists, and the best anesthesiologists together in the same room. On a routine appendectomy you'll rarely see that combination: we all say we want "the best doctor," but the best doctor's time is scarce, and it's probably best for his time to be spent working on crucial surgeries as part of a high-quality team. The very best will be collected together, and the very best team will be vastly more productive—more successful, faster, safer—than the tenth or twentieth best team.

The power of the O-ring is even stronger when the production process is more complicated: the more links there are in the chain, the easier it is to break. In *Star Trek III: The Search for Spock*, the Enterprise is trying to escape another Federation ship. Scotty, the engineer of the Enterprise, had been on the pursuing ship a little earlier. When the Enterprise jumps to warp speed, the pursuing ship tries to do the same, but sputters to a halt. Back on the Enterprise, Scotty pulls some electronic gadget out of his pocket and turns to Captain Kirk: "The more they overthink the plumbing, the easier it is to stop up the drain." The longer the chain of production, the easier it is to break the links.

The math proving that longer chains are more fragile is simple enough: one-half squared is a fourth, but one-half to the tenth power is basically zero. In long production processes, getting each step right is essential. If your laptop's battery and screen and eight other critical pieces each work 99 percent of the time, you've only got a 90 percent chance of a working laptop. The longer the chain of production, the bigger the exponent, and the bigger the payoff to finding even slightly more reliable workers.

And of course, not everything is O-ring: sometimes you can just throw enough person-hours at a problem and things will work out reasonably well—lawnmowing comes to mind, or perhaps routine food preparation or run-of-the-mill divorce paperwork or grading homework in an introductory economics course. But while O-rings aren't literally everywhere—a point we return to in the next chapter—they're still astonishingly common, especially at the cutting edge of the economy.

Evidence for O-Rings

The power of the O-ring analogy is that it shows how small differences in worker skill—along any dimension—can lead to big differences in who works together, what they produce, and how much they earn. The best data on the topic probably come from research into U.S. factories: workers at the most productive factories tend to earn more than those at less productive factories. Little surprise there: if you want to produce a lot of output, you probably have to pay to get higher-quality workers—people who show up on time, pay attention to detail, and work well in teams—and workers with more skills usually cost more. In a classic paper economists Davis and Haltiwanger reported that "many forms of skill complementarities across workers lead to ability sorting across plants" so that more-skilled workers end up together in the same firm.[2]

There's another reason to think that when workers are on team projects, we'll see a lot more output when the best are paired with the best: because workers inspire and motivate each other, for good and for ill. Humans pay attention to what's going on around them, and tend, even unconsciously, to imitate the behaviors they see. What's more, they do it quickly enough that a researcher can see the imitation in real time. A classic study on the topic looked at grocery checkout clerks. Since computers are recording each and every step of the checkout process—including which clerk is doing the checkout at which terminal—it's easy to see which clerks are more productive than others, who takes longer, who gets it done flawlessly and quickly. One can imagine that grocery stores care about such information, and indeed they do.

But Berkeley economists Alexandre Mas and Enrico Moretti did something else with that information: they checked to see if workers became more productive when they were put onto a shift with the top clerks, and if they became less productive when put onto a shift with the weaker clerks.[3] Perhaps it's no surprise that on average clerks rose (or descended) to the occasion: just being placed on a shift with other workers who were 10 percent more productive made a worker 1.5 percent more productive on that shift. But the authors wanted to see just *which* channel drove the motivation. Was it more important to *see* the better, more productive clerks, or was it more important to *be seen* by better clerks? Since the authors knew the setup of the grocery store, they could examine this: the checkout stands were oriented so that clerks could only easily see in one direction while working, and the researchers knew which aisle each clerk was at. So they asked a simple question: Were clerks motivated (or demotivated) by the workers behind them? The answer was a clear and resounding *yes*: if you were being watched by a more productive clerk, you became more productive yourself. And when you were being watched by someone who was less productive, you tended to slack off a little. Being watched mattered. When it came to productivity, the eyes had it.

Perhaps this is little surprise: swimmers and runners and athletes of all types know that you're a bit more likely to train harder when you're in the presence of stronger athletes. You swim a bit harder when the person in the next lane is swimming faster than you, whether you notice it consciously or not. And this doesn't just show up in grocery stores: another study found the same result with workers picking fruit, and lab experiments have confirmed similar findings with college students.[4]

That means that a slightly more productive employee can be a treasure. Not only does he produce more himself, but if he makes his colleagues even *slightly* more productive on average, then his own narrow contribution as a worker might actually be less important than his value as a motivator to many others. And remember: on a team, we are, each of us, potential motivators. So the bigger the team, the bigger the motivational side effect.

Of course, many skills matter, only some of which are captured by IQ tests. But academic management researchers have run dozens of studies checking to see if higher-average-IQ teams are more productive than lower-average-IQ teams. Indeed, enough studies of whether team IQ predicts team productivity have been run that psychologists Dennis Devine and Jennifer Philips ran a meta-analysis on the link between the two.[5] Unsurprisingly, the average IQ of team members does indeed predict team productivity across about two dozen studies. Average IQ mattered weakly in relatively realistic, workplace-type experiments and moderately in more formal psychology-laboratory-type tasks. In addition, average team cognitive skill appeared to matter more than the team high or team low, although the difference wasn't dramatic. My presumption is that the question of which IQ score matters most—the team high, team low, or team average—will vary from task to task. The more O-ring the process the more that the weakest team member's IQ score will matter. So, for instance, if everyone is required to participate, then everybody's skill set will matter. By contrast, if it's team chess, with Team A against Team B, it's easy enough to just figure out which team member is best at chess and let her take the lead most of the time.

Psychologist Christopher Chabris and his coauthors looked at team efforts another way: they checked to see if there was a da Vinci Effect for teams, a tendency for teams that did well on one kind of task such as a team game of checkers to do well on another task such as taking an IQ test as a team.[6] Indeed, they found a team da Vinci Effect, which they called a *c* factor, presumably in homage to the general or *g* factor of human intelligence. And what predicted which teams did better overall? The strongest two factors were whether team members routinely took turns speaking and how well team members did on a test of reading the emotions of others—the latter being a kind of emotional intelligence test. But nevertheless, the IQ of the average group member and the IQ of the highest-scoring group member were weak but still notable predictors of group intelligence, of c, and differences in individual IQ explained over one-third of differences in actual team performance.

Beyond O-Rings and Peers

The link between team productivity and team IQ is notable enough that one should sift through the ideas of economic theorists and sociologists to see what else might be at work besides peer effects and O-rings. Two influential ideas in recent economic theory are worth our attention: the theory of cheap talk, created by UC San Diego's Joel Sobel and Vincent Crawford,[7] and the theory of endogenous network formation, associated with Stanford's Matthew Jackson.[8]

Jackson's theory of networks starts with the obvious points that some human relationships are more valuable than others and that relationships are expensive to create. More important, he notes that in many cases it's valuable to get connected to people who already have a lot of connections—this is true when making friends in elementary school or when managing a large electronics firm. It's good to have connections for both personal and professional reasons: a good manager needs to keep the pulse of his firm, and a kid in school can use a coalition of friends to keep the loneliness at bay. Once one starts thinking about the value of connections, of relationships, it becomes obvious that cognitive skills are going to be a key ingredient in building good networks. Remembering the names of distant acquaintances, recalling the time that the company found someone to supply those specialized hard drives at the last minute, figuring out that Carlos in accounting has just the skill set that Marjorie in the executive suite was looking for in an executive VP—these are all skills that will be more common among people with higher IQ scores. The fact that intelligence is a form of social intelligence means that teams of workers with good test scores are—probably, not certainly—going to be better at building productive networks, at passing along information within the network accurately, and at finding possibilities for win-win outcomes.

You know the game of Telephone: kids sit in a circle, the first person whispers a slightly complicated phrase such as "The kittens go to the vet at 5 p.m. Sunday" into the ear of the child on her right. That child whispers what he hears to the person on his right, and so on around the room, with small errors accumulating until the first kid is finally told "The kids go to the Fabian Soap Derby." Corporations, government agencies, nonprofits—all are playing games of Telephone on a daily basis. Personally, I'd love to see a study of whether higher-IQ teams are better at Telephone than teams with average IQ. At this point in the academic literature, when we know that working memory is one of the better predictors of IQ, I'm willing to bet on how such a study would turn out.

The results of such a study would matter for creating successful organizations. One of the great insights of sociology is that in most organizations, the informal networks matter as much as the formal organization chart: things get done because of healthy networks, healthy cultures, healthy information flows. Teams with high test scores tend to have the skills to create these cultures, networks, and flows. The link between human capital and organizational success shows up in team experiments in the lab and in the routine finding that the most productive corporations tend to hire the most skilled workers. Matthew Jackson's theory of network formation reminds us that informal networks are like a campfire: every hot ember heats the other embers. Networks are yet another IQ multiplier.

Cheap Talk

This chapter covered economic theories that might explain why teams with high average test scores tend to be more productive. In all of the cases so far we've had good reasons from economic and psychological experiments to believe that there really are links in the chain running from test scores to group outcomes: memory span, social intelligence, and pattern finding are probably key real-world channels that matter, though different skills surely matter in different settings. With this final theory, I push the envelope, drawing on one of the most important findings in information economics but extending it in the hope that future researchers will check to see if group IQ matters in this now-classic setting. This is the world of cheap talk, the world we live in on a regular basis.

People often wonder, "Why doesn't he just say what he means?" The question comes up when two people are dating, when politicians negotiate with each other, when a worker explains to her boss how things are going. Sobel and Crawford came up with a general explanation for predicting who will speak clearly, who will speak in a hard-to-decipher code, and who will just babble, making nonsensical, irrelevant sounds. The setup goes like this: two people, call them A and B, may or may not have a common interest. A can send a message to B ("Let's meet for dinner at eight tonight"), then B takes some kind of action (B goes to the movies instead), and then the game ends. This is a one-shot game, not the repeated games we've looked at before, and person A doesn't have any kind of carrot or stick to encourage B's action. A's message to B is just cheap talk, just chit-chat, no binding contracts.

The outcome of the game is simple, perhaps even obvious: when two people have more in common—perhaps they're on the same football team, trying to win the FIFA World Cup—A will tend to speak clearly to B. When they have no common interests—perhaps they are strangers, or even nations at war—A will speak in gibberish to B. The words might sound like they "mean things" to regular people, but there's no real relationship between today's words and tomorrow's actions. It's the middle cases that are most interesting: Sobel and Crawford prove that even if two players have an infinitely large language at their disposal—infinite numbers or words or even multiple languages—a rational player A who shares only a *partial* common interest with his fellow player B will use only a *partial* set of the messages at his disposal. He'll speak in a stilted language.

In the rich countries we see politicians talk this way all the time: there are only a few "policy stances" a senator can take, and she's considered either a "moderate," a "conservative," or a "progressive" with maybe a handful of other options. Even though she might hold sophisticated, nuanced views on Shakespeare or the Qing dynasty or the best way to train for a marathon, once she switches to her role of senator the subtlety drains away and she is reduced to speaking in clichés. Part of the reason for speaking in clichés is because that's what voters can most easily remember—voters pay little attention to politics most of the time, so branding is important—but part of the reason might be because she is sending a signal to other senators in both parties about how she's going to act, how her constituents see things back home, how the poll numbers look for her planned presidential run. She doesn't have precisely the same goals and aspirations as any of her fellow politicians, so *both she and the other senators* know that anything she says has to be taken with a grain of salt. And actually, that's a good way to sum up Sobel and Crawford's finding: when two people in any kind of short-run interaction have diverging interests, both sides know that any statement gets taken with a grain of salt and act accordingly. There is no point in writing a ten-page essay that won't be believed.

So far, the skill of the two players—their test scores, their working memory, however you measure it—hasn't come into play at all. And indeed, in Sobel and Crawford's model, player skill doesn't come up. But I want to push beyond the formal model to suggest that people with high average test scores are more likely to convert a game of conflict into a game of cooperation. It would be a tragedy—worse, it would be a case of money left on the table—if two players couldn't find a way to redefine, to reimagine their conflict as a possibility for a win-win outcome. Two reasonably intelligent people getting divorced certainly face a zero-sum game when it comes to how they split up the retirement savings. And certainly, the divorcing spouses have little reason to tip their hands to each other about their bargaining strategy. But part of the power of memory, part of the power of being able to recall obscure facts, is the power to remember interests the couple still have in common: "Oh, there's a day care right between our two houses," "Here's an investment company that doesn't add on fees when we split our retirement plans in half," "I read about a job online that might be a good fit for you." There's at least the opportunity to think win-win.

It's not that higher-IQ individuals are nicer than other people—they aren't, as far as modern personality tests can tell us. It's that the memory skills and other traits that higher-IQ individuals tend to have are useful in searching out win-win possibilities, so it would be a great surprise if that didn't happen in the lab and out in the real world. And if a game of pure conflict turns even slightly into a game of mutual interest, Sobel and Crawford would predict that mutual interest will spur clearer communication.

Adam Smith's Pin Factory: A Team Effort

If you've never read it before, right now is an excellent time to read the first chapter of Adam Smith's second book, *The Wealth of Nations*, published in 1776. Just a few pages long, it discusses how pins are made—the small pushpins that have a flat head, not sewing needles or wooden clothespins. This chapter is where Smith lays out the power of the division of labor, showing that by dividing the job of making pins into about a half-dozen separate tasks—wire-cutting, point-sharpening, head-flattening, and so on—a small group of individuals could make a few pounds of pins each day. If instead each worker tried to do all the steps himself (the workers were all male in Smith's example) it would've been difficult for a worker to make even a few dozen low-quality pins each day. Dividing up the job makes the average worker far more productive.

Economists have reacted in different ways to Smith's observation: Marx looked at the pin factory and saw workers alienated from the craft process, for instance. A second way to look at the pin factory is to see an O-ring process at work, in which one weak worker means you're making pounds of shoddy pins each day. A third way is to see peer effects when a talented new worker ever so subtly inspires others to work just a little bit harder. And a worker with a good memory for names might know who would be a good fit for the opening in the pin-packing department. Production is a team effort, and teams with better-than-average memories, better-than-average social intelligence, and better-than-average job skills can become vastly more productive than even a slightly less-skilled team.

But there's a problem that's been in the background for this entire chapter: if higher team IQ makes a team vastly more productive, then why is it that within a country the higher-IQ workers earn only slightly more than workers with lower IQ scores? If markets are even halfway decent at tying wages to productivity, won't the higher-IQ workers earn vastly more? Isn't the weak relationship between IQ and wages evidence that IQ isn't that important or at least that O-rings aren't that important? In the next chapter, we'll see that these puzzles *can* be resolved, and the resolution gives reason to think that immigrants who come to rich countries with few marketable skills are to be welcomed.

Chapter 9

THE ENDLESS QUEST FOR SUBSTITUTES AND THE ECONOMIC BENEFITS OF IMMIGRATION

THE O-RING STORY EXPLAINS TOO MUCH. If real-world production processes were always so delicate that a minor error would destroy their value, and if the workers within a country really did wind up sorted into high-skill and low-skill firms, then less-skilled workers would be receiving only a tiny fraction of the pay of highly skilled workers. Inequality would be massive, the payoff to skill would be massive. But as we've seen from the Introduction onward, the payoff to IQ, to test scores, to any conventional measure of worker skill just isn't all that high within a country. Kremer's story about delicate O-ring production processes must capture something important, but it can't be the whole story. If O-rings are real, some other production processes must be equally real, some other kinds of jobs must be out there, jobs in which less-skilled workers can perform *almost* as well as more-skilled workers and earn *almost* as much as the more skilled. What might these kinds of jobs look like?

It turns out that mainstream economists have a pretty good story for what those kinds of jobs look like. Our benchmark economic model, the one we all learn the first year of graduate school, shows how workers with a little more skill can earn just a little more. The formal name is the Cobb-Douglas production function, but I call it the Foolproof sector of the economy. In a paper I wrote a few years ago I created a mathematical model that showed what happens if some parts of the economy are O-ring, in which team skills matter a lot, and other parts of the economy are Foolproof, in which less-skilled workers are just about as useful as top-of-the-line staff.[1] This model, a dramatic oversimplification of real-world economies, might help explain why people with high test scores typically earn only a little more than their average neighbors within a country but why *nations* with high average test scores earn vastly more than nations with just ordinary scores. The model helps explain why it's great to be a lower-scoring fish in a higher-scoring pond.

The O-Ring Sector Meets the Foolproof Sector

It goes like this. There are two kinds of tasks: delicate O-ring jobs and rough-and-tumble Foolproof jobs. The O-ring jobs we've seen already are tasks such as manufacturing microchips or coming up with merger plans for two big corporations or expertly landscaping a huge estate. Foolproof jobs are, well, foolproof: throw enough people at them and eventually you'll get the job done. Examples would be making $10 watches, or, as I suggested earlier, writing up routine divorce documents or mowing a typical suburban lawn.

O-ring jobs capture the "commanding heights" of the economy such as high tech agriculture or cutting-edge medicine, while Foolproof jobs control the vast plains such as subsistence farming or routine blood pressure checkups. O-ring jobs make great use of the best people to shape the way we live, while Foolproof jobs take up the slack, offering employment opportunities when nothing else is all that promising. And one final major difference: in the O-ring sector of the economy, twice the people mean twice the output at the same wages, but in the Foolproof sector, more people mean diminishing returns, more people mean wages get pushed down, down, down.

So here's one scenario. Imagine all workers in the same country have exactly the same skill set, a nation of clones. This is an oversimplification, but it'll help as a finger exercise. In this world, how would people decide to work in the O-ring sector rather than the Foolproof sector? How would the invisible hand of the market nudge workers in one direction or the other? The answer draws on one of the best ideas in economics, the law of one price, or LOOP. The LOOP says that as long as two precisely identical products are for sale, every consumer buys the cheaper product, and as long as two precisely identical jobs are available, every worker accepts the higher-paying job. This is an obvious enough point, but it has a surprising implication: if everybody follows the LOOP then nobody buys the more expensive good and nobody accepts the lower-paying job. And so either high-priced stores cut their prices or low-priced stores raise their prices or (more likely) some combination of the two happens. Yes, you can think of plenty of real-world exceptions, but the price of gas at stations across the street from each other rarely differs by more than a few cents, and that's not because of a government decree. If it differed by more than a few pennies per gallon almost everyone would go to the cheaper station. The LOOP doesn't take a stand on whether it's price cuts by the expensive shop or price hikes by the cheaper store that push the prices together, because of course that'll be different in different situations. But as long as the products (such as a worker's labor services) are selling on an open market, and as long as buyers (such as a business hiring a worker) can easily switch suppliers, then the LOOP is a strong force that can't be ignored. Prices get pushed together by an invisible hand of self-interest, by bargain seeking.

And so it will happen between the O-ring and the Foolproof sectors: if the two sectors paid noticeably different wages then workers would switch to the higher-paying sector, pushing up wages in the sector they left and driving down wages in the sector they moved to. So in a simple economy in which all workers have the same fairly high skill level the real question is what will wages be for the average worker? And as so often in economics, the answer depends on technology. If the O-ring sector is highly productive, then almost all the workers will end up in that sector, with only a few stragglers working in the Foolproof sector. After all, Foolproof is the land of diminishing returns, a part of the economy in which more competition drives down wages, so if new, equally skilled workers show up, they'll surely prefer the O-ring sector's stable wages.

But what if just one thing were changed: average worker skill? What if the O-ring sector was *in principle* highly productive but your nation didn't currently have high test scores or high education levels? Where would the workers wind up then? Many more would wind up in the Foolproof sector, in the land of routine jobs, of ordinary well-defined tasks that have probably been done for decades if not centuries. A company taking on an O-ring task with modestly skilled workers is a recipe for disaster: if it takes on tough tasks such as building jet airliners or computer chips it'll have to pour endless hours into quality control and repair and will probably end up just taking on less ambitious projects—tasks that are more routine, more Foolproof. Less-skilled workers *can* take on O-ring tasks, just not very productively. And since wages follow productivity, it's likely that less-skilled workers would pile into the Foolproof sector, driving wages down to the low average level in the O-ring sector.

And that's the first big prediction of the O-ring-Foolproof model: if one were to compare across countries that differ in average skill level, in nations of high average skill level—measured how you will—one will tend to see a bigger fraction of the workers in delicate, cutting-edge O-ring tasks and a smaller fraction of workers engaged in routine decades-old work tasks. A second prediction of the O-ring-Foolproof model comes when we ask what would happen if a few slightly less-skilled workers entered the country. The classic example, a common discussion topic in the rich countries today, is immigration of less-skilled workers from lower-average-skill-level countries. How does less-skilled immigration change the economy in the O-ring-Foolproof model?

In the simplest case, it really doesn't change the economy much. While less-skilled workers are poor substitutes for more-skilled workers in the O-ring sector, lower and higher skill levels are great substitutes for each other in the Foolproof sector. In the Foolproof sector you might be able to handle a dozen routine divorce cases with five fantastic lawyers or with seven or eight average lawyers; in the Foolproof sector you can have eight great cashiers running the checkout lines or you could have ten average cashiers. Again, the law of one price—and its close friend, pay for performance—will be at work in the Foolproof sector, so the average cashiers will earn a bit less than the best ones. In real life, that might happen through bonuses, promotions, or overtime pay for the better workers. However, the pay difference will be small compared to the vast differences in wages we'd see if the less-skilled workers had to use the risky O-ring technology.

So less-skilled workers will wind up in the Foolproof sector, but what becomes of the average workers? Do their wages get pushed down because of the competition? That's a possibility in this model—and it's a possibility in real life. But there's another possibility worth thinking about, one that captures something I *think* I see in the real world and something that recycles that great economic idea, the law of one price. The possibility: that the additional less-skilled workers push the average workers right over to the O-ring sector. Less-skilled immigration doesn't have to push the average worker into unemployment. Instead, the less-skilled immigrants drive the average-skilled workers into delicate O-ring work. The reason is simple: highly-skilled workers have good options in both sectors, and especially in a global economy in which output can be sold the world over, there's always room for one more skilled worker on one more assembly line or in one more cubicle farm. In my simple model the change happens instantly and efficiently, but of course in real life things aren't quite so simple, so we'll have to see further on what data-driven economists have found on the question of how less-skilled immigration affects the wages of long-standing citizens.

But the simple model has a simple prediction for an intuitive reason: as long as the O-ring technology is available—a technology that doesn't run into diminishing returns, a technology that is at its best when it has a skilled workforce—and as long as highly skilled workers are at work in both sectors, a rise in the number of less-skilled workers has *no effect* on high-skill wages and hence *no effect* on low-skill wages. The extra workers just move highly skilled workers back into the O-ring fields and the law of one price remains intact.

And of course, since in real life less-skilled immigrants tend to come from desperately poor countries, from nations with low average productivity, then even though these immigrants are earning lower wages than the average person in their new country, they're simultaneously earning vastly more than they would if they had stayed back in their home country. The O-ring-Foolproof model has an explanation for why that is: in the country with higher average skills, vastly more workers are working at O-ring tasks and relatively fewer are working at Foolproof jobs, so diminishing returns are weak in the Foolproof sector. But back in their less-skilled home country vastly more workers are crowded into the Foolproof sector, and fierce labor competition and diminishing returns are combining to drive down wages. And while in the rich countries Foolproof-sector work might consist of cleaning houses, working as home health aides, or cooking fast food, in the poor countries it's more likely to be subsistence farming, exceptionally dangerous mining, or running the most basic of retail shops. The O-ring-Foolproof story can explain why modest differences in average skills matter so much across countries, why those same modest differences might matter so little within a country, and why less-skilled immigrants get such a massive pay increase when they're allowed to migrate from a less-skilled to a more-skilled country. The O-ring-Foolproof story gets quite a lot of mileage out of a simple model.

How Low-Skilled Immigration Could (Possibly) Drive Down Wages

What happens if so many less-skilled immigrants arrive that they take up all of the previous Foolproof jobs? Then we're back in the world of commonsense economics: at that point, a rise in the supply of labor really would drive down the wages of less-skilled domestic workers. At that point, extra less-skilled workers really are competing against each other. They can't just nudge the more-skilled competition into the O-ring jobs because all the highly skilled workers already have O-ring jobs. So for modest degrees of less-skilled immigration, the model predicts zero effect on less-skilled wages, while if less-skilled immigration increases enough, then less-skilled home-country workers legitimately would have something to fear from the competition.

With this model in mind let's take a look at the evidence. What does less-skilled immigration do to the wages of what economists refer to as "native" home-country workers? For the rich countries, especially for the well-studied United States, the answer is clear: less-skilled immigration doesn't do much to the wages of U.S.-born residents. The most pessimistic academic estimates come from Harvard economists George Borjas and Larry Katz, who reported that less-skilled immigration may have pushed down the wages of American high school dropouts by 8 percent.[2] That's a real loss—I would be upset if I had to take an 8 percent wage cut—but remember, it's the most pessimistic of the serious estimates. It's more common to find zero effect or effects that are so close to zero that it's hard to tell one way or the other. It's even possible that economists Ottaviano and Peri are right: they claim that less-skilled immigration to the United States has actually raised the wages of the vast majority of U.S.-born workers.[3] Ottaviano and Peri's story is built around the idea of the division of labor: recent waves of less-skilled immigrants tend to have, for instance, relatively weak English-language skills. For that and other reasons—in the authors' words, because of different abilities in "language, quantitative skills, relationship skills and so on"—they're not in direct competition with U.S.-born, less-skilled, less-educated workers. In this view the people in the United States hurt most by recent waves of non-native-English-speaking immigrants are actually people who came as part of previous waves of non-native-English-speaking immigrants. Recent immigrants and older immigrants are substitutes for each other. Non-native English speakers tend to compete with each other for jobs, while U.S.-born English speakers, even those with limited job skills, have sizable areas of the labor market in which they face little direct competition from immigrants.

That's Ottaviano and Peri's model—only a model, like my own—but after testing their model on recent U.S. data they conclude that wages of U.S.-born citizens are probably about 1 percent higher as a result of recent immigration. Even U.S.-born workers lacking a high school diploma are predicted to benefit, with wages rising by 1 or 2 percent. Taken together, immigration is a slight boon and not a peril in Ottaviano and Peri's estimation. Ottaviano and Peri's facts match their model, at least for the level of immigration that the United States has experienced in recent years. And while Borjas and his coauthors have criticized Ottaviano and Peri's methods, the gap between Borjas and the Ottaviano-Peri views on the effects of less-skilled immigration is fairly small, much smaller than you'd expect if you read the heated public debates about less-skilled immigration across the rich countries.[4]

Economists and Immigration: A Rare Consensus

About a decade ago, dozens of American economists signed an open letter in support of more immigration. The letter touched on many points: that less-skilled immigrants appear to push down the wages of U.S.-born citizens little if at all, that immigration helps rich-country economies in ways that don't show up in official statistics, and that the biggest beneficiaries of less-skilled immigration are the immigrants themselves, whose lives are often transformed from a nightmare of dollar-a-day poverty to a realm of modest comfort, health, and safety. The diplomatically crafted letter, circulated by the Independent Institute, was signed by economists on the left and the right. I've always been glad I signed this letter: it sums up the great promise of immigration.[5] It's always worth reminding citizens of the high-productivity countries that immigration is still the most reliable way to raise the living standards of people in low-productivity countries. Rather then send aid workers or cash to help people in poor countries, the people of the rich countries could just allow people in poor countries to leave poor countries. Economists have run endless experiments checking to see if mosquito nets or better schools raise well-being in poor countries, and sometimes it looks like these interventions help a bit, but nobody questions whether people are better off when they move from dollar-a-day regions of the world to France or Germany or South Korea. It's obvious that voluntary migration cures the deepest poverty. For people who care about ending the deepest poverty, migration should be at the top of the list of potential cures.

A Tragic Tension: Will Freer Immigration Weaken Good Political Systems?

The key question is how many low-skilled immigrants a nation can take in and still keep a good politics.

Tyler Cowen[6]

The economics of less-skilled immigration to richer, more productive countries are reasonably clear: life-changing good news for the immigrant with only fairly small effects one way or the other on so-called "native" less-skilled workers. That's true when we look at the short run or when we look across towns and cities within the same country. And crucially, these studies hold politics aside and assume that less-skilled immigrants don't have an effect on a high-skill nation's government institutions. But if there's something we've seen in previous chapters, if there's something we've seen in Bryan Caplan's work on the link between voter education and voter beliefs, if there's something we've seen in the cross-country studies that find that higher national average test scores tend to predict lower average levels of corruption and in the philosophical debates over epistocracy, it's that good politics appears to depend on reasonably well-informed citizens. With this we come to a central tension of immigration among the currently less-skilled: the possible—I emphasize *possible*—effect on long-run institutions. Will less-skilled immigrants tend to vote for policies that will weaken the wealth-creating opportunities they've enjoyed? Or will less-skilled immigrants and their descendants instead build up high levels of human capital, perhaps raising the average information levels of voters? Conversely, might more-skilled immigrants bring a focus on the long run, a more informed perspective, into political discussions?

These important questions have been little studied. In a related context, Caplan has said,

> Most immigrants come from countries that are less free than the United States. . . . If enough statists come, won't our democracy switch to the kinds of policies that immigrants struggle to escape?[7]

Caplan goes on to argue that immigrants from less-free countries are likely to adopt the political norms and attitudes of their new countries, partly out of status-quo bias: immigrants are likely to conform at least modestly to the attitudes of their new fellow citizens. But he doesn't claim that new immigrants will completely conform to their new country:

> My point is not that status quo bias completely negates the effect of country of origin on political opinions. My point, rather, is that

status quo bias makes the political externality of immigration less negative than it appears.[8]

The question of how immigrants and their descendants will tend to influence the political institutions of their new homes is tremendously important: governments are made by people, after all. And since immigration by the currently less-skilled will likely be part of the future of the world's rich economies, I sincerely hope that the rich countries will find deep and effective ways to raise the human capital, the education levels, and the test scores of all of these nations' citizens and all of their immigrants. Our future may depend upon it.

Chapter 10

POEM AND CONCLUSION

The Hive Mind: A Summary

Patient savers
Skilled team members
On the average
   Prudent Peers

Open minded
Informed Voters
Pretty good co-operators
On the average
With exceptions
Quite productive
   Prudent Peers

Whose Skills Matter Most for Productivity?

One recurring question people have asked me over the years is, do the cognitive skills of the top 5 or 10 percent of the population matter more than the nation's average skill level? I didn't have an answer to this question until Rindermann and his coauthors created cognitive skill estimates for each nation's top performers, based heavily on the PISA and TIMSS international tests mentioned in the Introduction. For instance, they estimated the cognitive skills of the top 5 percent of the population in dozens of nations. In Rindermann's estimates and in those of others, the best guess is that the cognitive skill of elites really does matter more than the nation's average score.

And when it comes to institutional quality, Potrafke and I found that the cognitive skills of the top 5 percent did the better job of predicting property-rights-friendly institutions, although the nation's average score also did a reasonably good job as a predictor. However, it's worth keeping in mind that countries with high average test scores almost always have high average test scores among the top 5 percent, so the statistical tests that all of us have performed aren't in a great position to sort out the question definitively. I hope that future work will help answer the question of which group matters more for the economy's long-run health, but for the time being it's reasonable to start with the belief that a nation's top performers matter more for the economy than a nation's average performers.

At the same time, it's reasonable to think through for yourself the question of whether and why top performers might matter more than the typical person. Would they set an example of frugality that others would follow? Would they have disproportionate control over the political process? Would they be the positive reciprocators that help spur others both at work and in political life to reach for the Coasian win-win outcome? All of these channels are worth thinking about, and I hope you'll do just that. But there may be more we can do.

The Best Way to Raise National Average IQ: A Mystery Worth Solving

By now you've seen how important it is to raise test scores in every country: the skills that help people do well on an IQ test help them across their entire lives. And of course there's a major difference, an overwhelming difference, between genuinely raising broad-based cognitive skills versus just boosting one particular score on one particular standardized test. The tests don't matter: the skills do. If it's at all possible, let's find ways to raise broad-based mental skills in every country whether through public health interventions or educational advances. Let's search for policies that yield a da Vinci Effect, not just a higher score on one or two narrow skills such as arithmetic or vocabulary. It will probably take decades to see the full benefits of higher overall test scores, but the payoffs would be massive.

A Global Flynn Cycle: A Possibility Worth Striving For

Over a decade ago I began my research into how IQ matters for nations. I soon found that the strong link between average IQ and national productivity couldn't be explained with just the conventional finding that IQ predicts higher wages. IQ apparently mattered far more for nations than for individuals. In my early work, I estimated that IQ mattered about six times more for nations than for individuals: your nation's IQ mattered so much more than your own.

That puzzle, that paradox of IQ, is what set me on my intellectual journey, through the patience channel of Ramsey, the cooperation channel of Axelrod, the voting channel of Caplan, the O-ring channel of Kremer, the conformity channel of Asch. All of these channels are IQ multipliers, all show how the cognitive skills of your neighbors, your fellow citizens, shape your productivity in the long run. And perhaps even more important, if higher mental skills raise productivity and productivity raises health and health in turn raises mental skills, the IQ multiplier becomes a Flynn Cycle, in which small public health improvements cause long-lasting productivity gains. How long could the Flynn Cycle continue in lower-scoring countries? With our current state of knowledge, can health and nutrition and educational reforms raise IQ scores around the world to the average levels of East Asia? I don't know the answer to these questions, but it's worth trying to find out. Even if current knowledge only lets us close part of the cognitive skill gap across countries, it's a project worth embarking upon. Let's get to it.

DATA APPENDIX

Country	CA	IQ	Country	CA	IQ
Argentina	82	93	Italy	97	97
Armenia	93	92	Japan	105	105
Australia	101	98	Jordan	86	85
Austria	100	100	Kuwait	76	87
Bahrain	84	81	Lebanon	84	82
Belgium	99	99	Lithuania	97	91
Bosnia	91	94	Malaysia	96	92
Botswana	74	71	Malta	92	97
Brazil	82	87	Mexico	85	88
Bulgaria	93	93	Morocco	71	84
Canada	102	99	Netherlands	102	100
Chile	84	90	New Zealand	100	99
Colombia	81	84	Norway	96	100
Croatia	96	99	Oman	81	85
Czech Republic	100	98	Palestine	80	86
Denmark	98	98	Philippines	74	86
Egypt	81	83	Poland	97	95
Estonia	102	99	Portugal	92	95
Finland	103	99	Qatar	72	83
France	98	98	Romania	89	91
Germany	99	99	Russia	97	97
Ghana	61	71	Saudi Arabia	74	80
Greece	94	92	Singapore	105	108
Hong Kong	104	108	Slovakia	98	96
Hungary	99	97	Slovenia	99	96
Iceland	96	101	South Africa	63	72
Indonesia	82	87	South Korea	106	106
Iran	83	84	Spain	96	98
Ireland	100	92	Sweden	100	99
Israel	93	95	Switzerland	100	101

Country	CA	IQ	Country	CA	IQ
Syria	81	79	United Arab Emirates	92	83
Taiwan	103	105	United Kingdom	100	100
Thailand	90	91	United States	98	98
Tunisia	81	84	Uruguay	88	96
Turkey	87	90	Yemen	64	83
Ukraine	93	95			

Notes: The middle column reports the Rindermann, Sailer, Thompson cognitive ability (CA) scores estimated from the international tests the PISA, the TIMSS, and the PIRLS. The right-hand column reports national average IQ as estimated by Lynn and Meisenberg. The table only reports data for countries where both estimates are available.

Both estimates include data of varying quality; in particular, developing country estimates may be based on small samples or limited numbers of tests and should be treated with caution. This is a problem that also arises when measuring GDP per person in developing countries, as Morten Jerven's book *Poor Numbers* documents.

Sources: Rindermann, Sailer, and Thompson, "The Impact of Smart Fractions" and Lynn and Meisenberg, "National IQs Calculated." See also Jervens, *Poor Numbers*.

NOTES

Introduction

1. Covey, *Seven Habits of Highly Effective People*.
2. Barry and Friedman, "Bargainer Characteristics in Distributive and Integrative Negotiation."
3. Hanushek and Kimko, "Schooling, Labor-Force Quality, and the Growth of Nations."
4. Hanushek and Kimko, "Schooling," 1204.
5. Rindermann, Sailer, and Thompson, "The Impact of Smart Fractions." See also Rindermann and Thompson, "Cognitive Capitalism." Note that in Figure I.1 the cognitive ability estimates from this 2009 paper are compared to 2005 GDP per person. Since average test scores and GDP typically change little from year to year, the difference in years is immaterial when making cross-country comparisons. Also, the 2005 GDP data are actual estimates of 2005 GDP per person, while the 2009 estimates were published in 2009, on the basis of earlier data.
6. On the difficulties of measuring and the weaknesses in official statistics in less-developed countries, see Jerven, *Poor Numbers*; Young, "The African Growth Miracle"; and Nye and Moul, "The Political Economy of Numbers."
7. Jones and Schneider, "Intelligence, Human Capital, and Economic Growth." Others have run similar tests and found similar results, including Weede and Kämpf, "The Impact of Intelligence and Institutional Improvements on Economic Growth"; and Ram, "IQ and Economic Growth." The only peer-reviewed paper of which I am aware that does not find national average IQ to be a robust predictor of modern economic growth compares IQ against end-of-period education (for example, post-1999 secondary schooling): Moreale and Levendis, "IQ and Economic Development." But as Bils and Klenow note (in "Does Schooling Cause Growth?"), much or perhaps even most recent education is likely a result of predicted prosperity, not simply a cause of prosperity. This suggests that end-of-period education is poorly suited to be a regression control variable.

Chapter 1

1. Both the computer speed and the strength analogies are standard metaphors in discussions of intelligence research, as is the idea of using indirect methods to measure the *g* factors for computer speed and strength. I would welcome a canonical reference to either idea, but am aware of none.
2. Spearman, "'General Intelligence.'"
3. Mackintosh, *IQ and Human Intelligence*, 45. This is an excellent textbook.
4. Raven Matrix, *User: Life of Riley*.
5. Allison, Kaprio, Korkeila, Koskenvuo, Neale, and Hayakawa, "The Heritability of Body Mass Index."
6. Technical note: "nearly perfect" indicates a correlation with an absolute value of 0.9 or greater. All correlations are rounded to the nearest 0.1.
7. Dodrill, "Long-Term Reliability of the Wonderlic Personnel Test."
8. Allison and others, "Heritability of Body Mass Index."
9. These "strong" or "robust" relationships are correlations between 0.6 and 0.8 in absolute value.
10. "Modest" or "moderate" equals correlations of 0.3 to 0.5.
11. Stanovich, Cunningham, and Freeman, "Intelligence, Cognitive Skills, and Early Reading Progress."
12. Weinberg, Dietz, Penick, and McAlister, "Intelligence, Reading Achievement, Physical Size, and Social Class."
13. Mackintosh, *IQ and Human Intelligence*, 132.
14. Hunt, *Human Intelligence*, 201. This is a provocative and informed survey and interpretation of the literature.
15. Deary, *Intelligence*, 48. This is an excellent introduction to IQ research.
16. Hunt, *Human Intelligence*, 201.
17. Deary, *Intelligence*, 57.
18. Kranzler and Jensen, "Inspection Time and Intelligence."
19. Schmidt and Hunter, "The Validity and Utility of Selection Methods in Personnel Psychology." See a graphical version of their famous Table 1 in Hunt, *Human Intelligence*, 331.
20. Hunt, *Human Intelligence*, 333.
21. Hunt, *Human Intelligence*, 334.
22. McHenry, Hough, Toquam, Hanson, and Ashworth, "Project A Validity Results." See Table 4, cited in Hunt, *Human Intelligence*, 331.
23. Zax and Rees, "IQ, Academic Performance, Environment, and Earnings."
24. Bowles, Gintis, and Osborne, "The Determinants of Earnings."
25. Strenze, "Intelligence and Socioeconomic Success."
26. Mackintosh, *IQ and Human Intelligence*, 242.

27. Mackintosh, *IQ and Human Intelligence*, 242–243.//
28. Mackintosh, *IQ and Human Intelligence*, 250.

Chapter 2

1. Psychological research into test bias is an entire field of study. An early, still widely cited work is Arthur Jensen's *Bias in Mental Testing*. The currently best-known form of possible test bias is *stereotype threat*. In a stereotype threat scenario, students from a particular demographic group tend to perform poorly on a test after being reminded of the cultural stereotypes about their group's average performance on that type of test. According to classic studies, female students perform worse on math tests after being reminded beforehand of a cultural stereotype that females are supposedly weaker than males at math. Similar tests have been run comparing African-American student test performance in scenarios in which stereotypes are invoked beforehand versus scenarios in which stereotypes are not invoked. The vast literature is too large to summarize here, but Hunt's textbook (*Human Intelligence*) and Nisbett's coauthored paper (Nisbett and others, "Intelligence: New Findings and Theoretical Developments") both attempt to do so. The latter paper notes that a then-new meta-analysis reports "a conservative estimate that women's math performance and Black students' verbal performance are suppressed by about 0.2 [standard deviations]" although in some studies the effect is five times larger. Most would consider 0.2 standard deviations a small to moderate effect. A newer meta-analysis by Flore and Wicherts of studies of stereotype threat for females finds about the same effect size; see "Does Stereotype Threat Influence Performance of Girls in Stereotyped Domains?" And Hunt's text notes that test score gaps between demographic groups tend to shrink when the tests have high stakes, such as in college examination settings. The stereotype threat literature has been deeply intellectually invigorating; however it does not currently appear to explain the entirety or even the majority of test score gaps across demographic groups.

2. Mackintosh, *IQ and Human Intelligence*, 326.

3. Lynn and Vanhanen, *IQ and the Wealth of Nations*.

4. Lynn and Vanhanen, *IQ and Global Inequality*; Lynn and Meisenberg, "National IQs Calculated and Validated for 108 Nations."

5. Eppig, Fincher, and Thornhill, "Parasite Prevalence and the Worldwide Distribution of Cognitive Ability."

6. *The Economist*, "Mens Sana in Corpore Sano"; Gates, "Annual Letter from Bill Gates: 2011."

7. Georgas, van de Vijver, and Saklofske, *Culture and Children's Intelligence*.

8. Jones and Schneider, "IQ in the Production Function."

9. Wicherts, Dolan, and van der Maas, "A Systematic Literature Review of the Average IQ of Sub-Saharan Africans."

10. Wicherts, Dolan, and van der Maas, "A Systematic Literature Review"; Wicherts, Dolan, Carlson, and van der Maas, "Raven's Test Performance of Sub-Saharan Africans"; Wicherts, Dolan, Carlson, and van der Maas, "Another Failure to Replicate Lynn's Estimate of the Average IQ of Sub-Saharan Africans"; Wicherts, Dolan, and van der Maas, "The Dangers of Unsystematic Selection Methods and the Representativeness of 46 samples of African Test-Takers."

11. Lynn and Meisenberg, "The Average IQ of Sub-Saharan Africans."

12. Behrman, Alderman, and Hoddinott, "Hunger and Malnutrition." This paper contains other relevant citations on the link between cognitive skills and wages in less developed countries.

13. Iwawaki and Vernon, "Japanese Abilities and Achievements."

14. Hunt, *Human Intelligence*, 422.

15. Rindermann, "The g-Factor of International Cognitive Ability Comparisons."

16. Hendricks, "How Important Is Human Capital for Development?" and Jones and Schneider, "IQ in the Production Function."

17. Another possible major difference across countries is migrant self-selection. Hypothetically, perhaps migrants from some regions of the world are "best in class" while migrants from other regions are median performers. Hendricks runs two checks for this possibility: first, he shows, on the basis of studies from a variety of countries, that in the typical country emigrants don't differ after controlling for observable differences. Second, he reports studies of return migrants, individuals who left their home country and returned, and overall these return migrants tend to earn about the same as other citizens who never migrated. For my purposes, I should note that as long as all nations are about equally self-selected—for instance, if migrants to the United States tend to be, say, 20 percent more skilled than average—then that won't change my results. In high school algebra terms, such self-selection is a shift in the y-intercept, not a shift in the slope.

Chapter 3

1. Solon and others, "Associations Between Cognitive Function, Blood Lead Concentration, and Nutrition."

2. Hunt, *Human Intelligence*, 262.

3. Flynn, "Massive IQ Gains in 14 Nations."

4. Flynn, *Are We Getting Smarter? Rising IQ in the Twenty-First Century*, 12.

5. Flynn, "The 'Flynn Effect' and Flynn's Paradox," 857.

6. Flynn, *What Is Intelligence?* See also Flynn, *Are We Getting Smarter?*

7. Nisbett and others, "Intelligence: New Findings and Theoretical Developments."

8. Flynn, *Are We Getting Smarter?*, 36.

9. Macintosh, *IQ and Human Intelligence*, 300.
10. Nisbett, *Intelligence and How to Get It*, 184.
11. Hunt, *Human Intelligence*, 277.
12. Burkeman, review.
13. Hunt, *Human Intelligence*, 301–303; Mackintosh, *IQ and Human Intelligence*, 303–305.
14. Hunt, *Human Intelligence*, 301–303.
15. Mackintosh, *IQ and Human Intelligence*, 303–305.
16. Hoxby, "Peer Effects in the Classroom."
17. Christiakis and Fowler, *Connected*.
18. Burke and Sass, "Classroom Peer Effects and Student Achievement," 52.
19. A special 2013 issue of *Intelligence* focused on the Flynn Effect; many of the hypotheses listed here are noted throughout that issue and particularly in Williams, "Overview of the Flynn Effect."
20. McNeil, "In Raising the World's IQ, the Secret's in the Salt."
21. Gorman, "The Impact of Childhood Lead Exposure on Adult Crime," which offers a summary of Reyes, "Environmental Policy as Social Policy."
22. Nevin, "Understanding International Crime Trends."
23. Drum, "America's Real Criminal Element: Lead."
24. United Nations Environmental Program, "Sub-Saharan Africa Lead Matrix."

Chapter 4

1. Dohmen, Falk, Huffman, and Sunde, "Are Risk Aversion and Impatience Related to Cognitive Ability?"
2. Shamosh and Gray, "Delay Discounting and Intelligence."
3. Benjamin, Brown, and Shapiro, "Who Is Behavioral?"
4. Oechssler, Roider, and Schmitz, "Cognitive Abilities and Behavioral Biases."
5. Warner and Pleeter, "The Personal Discount Rate."
6. Shamosh and Gray, "Delay Discounting and Intelligence."
7. Ramsey, "A Mathematical Theory of Saving."
8. The savings rate is the IMF World Economic Outlook's "Gross national savings (Percent of GDP)." Savings is "gross disposable income less final consumption expenditure after taking account of an adjustment for pension funds," and both the numerator (savings) and the denominator (GDP) are measured in "current local currency." The data are averaged from 1980 to 2010, and the correlation is essentially unchanged if the median savings rate is used instead of the mean. The data are relatively complete, but in some cases the last few years of data are estimated by the IMF. Source of definition: International Monetary Fund, "World Economic Outlook Database."

9. Hamilton and Clemens, "Genuine Savings Rates in Developing Countries."
10. For example, Hoyer, MacInnis, and Pieters, *Consumer Behavior*.
11. Kuhn, Kooreman, Soetevent, and Kapteyn, "The Effects of Lottery Prizes on Winners and Their Neighbors."
12. I believe this is an old idea in the literature; I welcome relevant citations.
13. Barro and Sala-i-Martin, *Economic Growth*.
14. Lane and Milesi-Ferretti, "The External Wealth of Nations Mark II."
15. Jones, "Will the Intelligent Inherit the Earth?"
16. Hung and Qian, "Why Is China's Saving Rate So High?" 6.
17. Hung and Qian, "Why Is China's Savings Rate So High?" 33.
18. Jensen, "Agency Costs."
19. Gillette, "Can Public Debt Enhance Democracy?"

Chapter 5

1. Axelrod, *The Evolution of Cooperation*, 139.
2. Seabright, *The Company of Strangers*, 2.
3. Axelrod, *Evolution of Cooperation*.
4. Tit for tat has proven to be a great strategy, although in Axelrod's final tests tit for two tats did slightly better. That meant waiting until you get cheated on twice before punishing. After decades of subsequent RPD tournaments, the only one that *might* be better than those is *win-stay/lose-shift*, which is just what it sounds like: if you're getting a decent or excellent payment (joint cooperation or exploitation of someone who plays nice no matter what you do) then stick with that approach. But if you lost last time (because the other person defected), then change what you were doing.
5. Burks, Carpenter, Goette, and Rustichini, "Cognitive Skills Affect Economic Preferences."
6. Millet and Dewitte, "Altruistic Behavior as a Costly Signal of General Intelligence."
7. Putterman, Tyran, and Kamei, "Public Goods and Voting on Formal Sanction Schemes."
8. Burnham, Cesarini, Johannesson, Lichtenstein, and Wallace, "Higher Cognitive Ability Is Associated with Lower Entries in p Beauty Contest."
9. Brañas-Garza, García-Muñoz, and González, "Cognitive Effort in the Beauty Contest Game."
10. Segal and Hershberger, "Cooperation and Competition Between Twins." I eventually found one other paper in which the game lasted 150 rounds and the players were given the Wonderlic IQ test. Pair IQ had a statistically insignificant 0.1 correlation with cooperation. Terhune, "'Wash-In,' 'Wash-Out,' and Systemic Effects in Extended Prisoner's Dilemma."

11. Jones, "Are Smarter Groups More Cooperative? Evidence from Prisoner's Dilemma Experiments, 1959–2003." Also see Jones, "Are Smarter Groups More Cooperative? Results for Corrected and Extended Datasets."

12. al-Ubaydli, Jones, and Weel, "Cognitive Ability and Cooperation in the Prisoner's Dilemma."

13. In the academic literature "conditional cooperators" usually refers to people who cooperate when others are likely to be cooperating *and* who defect when others appear to be defecting. Our paper did not uncover a statistically significant greater tendency to defect when the other player defected, so our conditional cooperation is a form of positive reciprocity.

14. Chaudhuri, "Sustaining Cooperation in Laboratory Public Goods Experiments."

15. Bowles and Gintis, "Homo Reciprocans."

16. Proto, Rustichini, and Sofianos, "Higher Intelligence Groups Have Higher Cooperation Rates in the Repeated Prisoner's Dilemma."

17. Sharma, Bottom, and Elfenbein, "On the Role of Personality."

18. Seabright, *The Company of Strangers*, 54.

19. Kanazawa and Fontaine, "Intelligent People Defect More in a One-Shot Prisoner's Dilemma Game."

20. Among others, Mackintosh, *IQ and Human Intelligence*, 247.

Chapter 6

1. Knight, "Intellectual Confusion on Morals and Economics."
2. Axelrod, *Evolution of Cooperation*.
3. Rutter, *History of the Seventh (Service) Battalion*, 29, quoted in Axelrod, *Evolution of Cooperation*, 85.
4. Ordeshook, *Game Theory and Political Theory: An Introduction*.
5. Wittman, *The Myth of Democratic Failure*.
6. Buchanan, *The Limits of Liberty*, ix.
7. Roberts, "If You're Paying, I'll Have Top Sirloin."
8. Acemoglu, "Why Not a Political Coase Theorem?"
9. Buchanan, *Limits of Liberty*, p. 124.
10. Arrow, "Gifts and Exchanges."
11. Kydland and Prescott, "Rules Rather Than Discretion."
12. Barro and Gordon, "Rules, Discretion and Reputation in a Model of Monetary Policy."
13. Potrafke, "Intelligence and Corruption."
14. Jones and Potrafke, "Human Capital and National Institutional Quality."
15. Kanyama, "Quality of Institutions."
16. Rindermann, Sailer, and Thompson, "The Impact of Smart Fractions."

Chapter 7

1. Caplan, *The Myth of the Rational Voter*, 3.
2. Kraus, Malmfors, and Slovic. "Intuitive Toxicology," cited in Caplan, *Myth of the Rational Voter*.
3. Curran, Iyengar, Lund, and Salovaara-Moring, "Media System, Public Knowledge and Democracy."
4. Blinder and Krueger, "What Does the Public Know About Economic Policy?"
5. Caplan and Miller, "Intelligence Makes People Think Like Economists."
6. Kahan, Peters, Dawson, and Slovic, "Motivated Numeracy and Enlightened Self-Government."
7. Klein, "How Politics Makes Us Stupid."
8. Wolfinger, and Rosenstone, *Who Votes?*
9. Denny and Doyle, "Political Interest, Cognitive Ability and Personality"; Deary, Batty, and Gale. "Childhood Intelligence Predicts Voter Turnout."
10. Hauser, "Education, Ability, and Civic Engagement in the Contemporary United States."
11. Schoon, Cheng, Gale, Batty, and Deary, "Social Status, Cognitive Ability, and Educational Attainment."
12. Rindermann, Flores-Mendoza, and Woodley, "Political Orientations, Intelligence and Education."
13. Pande, "Can Informed Voters Enforce Better Governance?"
14. A reference to Carl Sagan's television series *Cosmos*.
15. Ferraz and Finan, "Electoral Accountability and Corruption."
16. Pande, "Can Informed Voters Enforce Better Governance?"
17. Asch, "Opinions and Social Pressure."
18. Asch, "Opinions and Social Pressure."
19. Noelle-Neumann, "The Spiral of Silence."
20. Nickerson, "Social Networks and Political Context."
21. Farrar, Green, Green, Nickerson, and Shewfelt, "Does Discussion Group Composition Affect Policy Preferences?"
22. Farrar and others, "Does Discussion Group Composition Affect Policy Preferences?" p. 637.
23. Cowgill, Wolfers, and Zitzewitz, "Using Prediction Markets to Track Information Flows." In particular, see Table 1.
24. Cowgill, Wolfers, and Zitzewitz, "Using Prediction Markets to Track Information Flows," 3.
25. Thomas Jefferson, "Letter to Charles Yancey."
26. Hochschild, "If Democracies Need Informed Voters," 119.
27. Hochschild, "If Democracies Need Informed Voters," 120.

28. Brennan, "The Right to a Competent Electorate."

Chapter 8

1. Kremer, "The O-Ring Theory of Economic Development."
2. Davis and Haltiwanger, "Wage Dispersion Between and Within US Manufacturing Plants," p. 131.
3. Mas and Moretti, "Peers at Work."
4. All cited in Mas and Moretti, "Peers at Work."
5. Devine and Philips, "Do Smarter Teams Do Better?"
6. Woolley, Chabris, Pentland, Hashmi, and Malone, "Evidence for a Collective Intelligence Factor in the Performance of Human Groups."
7. Crawford and Sobel, "Strategic Information Transmission."
8. Jackson, *Social and Economic Networks*.

Chapter 9

1. Jones, "The O-Ring Sector and the Foolproof Sector."
2. Borjas and Katz, "The Evolution of the Mexican-Born Workforce in the United States.
3. Ottaviano and Peri, "Rethinking the Effect of Immigration on Wages."
4. Borjas, Grogger, and Hanson, "Imperfect Substitution Between Immigrants and Natives."
5. Tabarrok and Theroux, "Open Letter on Immigration."
6. Cowen, "Assorted Links."
7. Caplan, "Why Should We Restrict Immigration?"
8. Caplan, "Why Should We Restrict Immigration?" p. 13.

BIBLIOGRAPHY

Acemoglu, Daron. "Why Not a Political Coase Theorem? Social Conflict, Commitment, and Politics." *Journal of Comparative Economics* 31, no. 4 (2003): 620–652.

Allison, David B., Jaakko Kaprio, Maarit Korkeila, Markku Koskenvuo, Michael C. Neale, and Kazuo Hayakawa. "The Heritability of Body Mass Index Among an International Sample of Monozygotic Twins Reared Apart." *International Journal of Obesity* 20, no. 6 (1996): 501–506.

al-Ubaydli, Omar, Garett Jones, and Jaap Weel. "Cognitive Ability and Cooperation in the Prisoner's Dilemma." Working paper, George Mason University, 2011.

Arrow, Kenneth J. "Gifts and Exchanges." *Philosophy & Public Affairs* 1, no. 4 (Summer 1972): 343–362.

Asch, Solomon. "Opinions and Social Pressure." *Readings About the Social Animal*, (1955): 17–26.

Axelrod, Robert M. *The Evolution of Cooperation*. New York: Basic Books, 2006.

Barro, Robert J., and David B. Gordon. "Rules, Discretion and Reputation in a Model of Monetary Policy." *Journal of Monetary Economics* 12, no. 1 (1983): 101–121.

Barro, Robert J., and Xavier Sala-i-Martin. *Economic Growth*. Cambridge: MIT Press, 2004.

Barry, Bruce, and Raymond A. Friedman. "Bargainer Characteristics in Distributive and Integrative Negotiation." *Journal of Personality and Social Psychology* 74 (1998): 345–359.

Behrman, Jere R., Harold Alderman, and John Hoddinott, "Hunger and Malnutrition." Paper presented at the Copenhagen Consensus—Challenges and Opportunities, Copenhagen, Denmark, February 19, 2004.

Benjamin, Daniel J., Sebastian A. Brown, and Jesse M. Shapiro. "Who Is Behavioral? Cognitive Ability and Anomalous Preferences." *Journal of the European Economic Association* 11, no. 6 (2013): 1231–1255.

Bils, Mark, and Peter J. Klenow, "Does Schooling Cause Growth?" *American Economic Review* 90 (2000): 1160–1183.

Blinder, Alan S., and Alan B. Krueger. "What Does the Public Know About Economic Policy, and How Does It Know It?" National Bureau of Economic Research working paper, no. w10787 (2004).

Borjas, George J., Jeffrey Grogger, and Gordon H. Hanson. "Imperfect Substitution Between Immigrants and Natives: A Reappraisal." National Bureau of Economic Research working paper, no. w13887 (2008).

Borjas, George J., and Lawrence F. Katz. "The Evolution of the Mexican-Born Workforce in the United States." In *Mexican Immigration to the United States*, ed. George J. Borjas, p. 13–56. Chicago: University of Chicago Press, 2007.

Bowles, Samuel, and Herbert Gintis. "Homo Reciprocans." *Nature* 415 (2002): 125–128.

Bowles, Samuel, Herbert Gintis, and Melissa Osborne. "The Determinants of Earnings: A Behavioral Approach." *Journal of Economic Literature* 39, no. 4 (2001): 1137–1176.

Brañas-Garza, Pablo, Teresa Garcia-Muñoz, and Roberto Hernán González. "Cognitive Effort in the Beauty Contest Game." *Journal of Economic Behavior & Organization* 83, no. 2 (2012): 254–260.

Brennan, Jason. "The Right to a Competent Electorate." *The Philosophical Quarterly* 61, no. 245 (2011): 700–724.

Buchanan, James. *The Limits of Liberty: Between Anarchy and Leviathan.* Chicago: University of Chicago Press, 1975.

Burke, Mary A., and Tim R. Sass. "Classroom Peer Effects and Student Achievement." *Journal of Labor Economics* 31, no. 1 (2013): 51–82.

Burkeman, Oliver. Review of "Scarcity: Why Having Too Little Means So Much," by Sendhil Mullainathan and Eldar Shafir, *The Guardian*, September 2013.

Burks, Stephen V., Jeffrey P. Carpenter, Lorenz Goette, and Aldo Rustichini. "Cognitive Skills Affect Economic Preferences, Strategic Behavior, and Job Attachment." *Proceedings of the National Academy of Sciences* 106, no. 19 (2009): 7745–7750.

Burnham, Terence C., David Cesarini, Magnus Johannesson, Paul Lichtenstein, and Björn Wallace. "Higher Cognitive Ability Is Associated with Lower Entries in p Beauty Contest." *Journal of Economic Behavior & Organization* 72, no. 1 (2009): 171–175.

Caplan, Bryan. *The Myth of the Rational Voter: Why Democracies Choose Bad Policies.* Princeton, NJ: Princeton University Press, 2008.

———. "Why Should We Restrict Immigration?" *Cato Journal* 32, no. 1 (Winter 2012): 12–13.

Caplan, Bryan, and Stephen C. Miller. "Intelligence Makes People Think Like Economists: Evidence from the General Social Survey." *Intelligence* 38, no. 6 (2010): 636–647.

Chaudhuri, Ananish. "Sustaining Cooperation in Laboratory Public Goods Experiments: A Selective Survey of the Literature." *Experimental Economics* (2011).

Christiakis, Nicholas, and James Fowler. *Connected: How Your Friends' Friends' Friends Affect Everything You Feel, Think, or Do*. New York: Little, Brown, 2011.

Covey, Steven. *The Seven Habits of Highly Effective People: Anniversary Edition*. New York: Simon & Schuster, 2013.

Cowen, Tyler. "Assorted Links." *Marginal Revolution*, May 25, 2013. marginalrevolution.com/marginalrevolution/2013/05/assorted-links-802.html, accessed February 8, 2015.

Cowgill, Bo, Justin Wolfers, and Eric Zitzewitz. "Using Prediction Markets to Track Information Flows: Evidence from Google." In *Auctions, Market Mechanisms and Their Applications*, ed. Sanmay Das, Michael Ostrovsky, David Pennock, and Boleslaw K. Szymanski, p. 3. New York: Springer, 2009.

Crawford, Vincent P., and Joel Sobel. "Strategic Information Transmission." *Econometrica: Journal of the Econometric Society* (1982): 1431–1451.

Curran, James, Shanto Iyengar, Anker Brink Lund, and Inka Salovaara-Moring. "Media System, Public Knowledge and Democracy: A Comparative Study." *European Journal of Communication* 24, no. 1 (2009): 5–26.

Davis, Steve J., and John Haltiwanger. "Wage Dispersion Between and Within US Manufacturing Plants, 1963–86." *Brookings Papers on Economic Activity. Microeconomics* (1991): 115–200.

Deary, Ian J. *Intelligence: A Very Short Introduction*. Oxford: Oxford University Press, 2001.

Deary, Ian J., G. David Batty, and Catharine R. Gale. "Childhood Intelligence Predicts Voter Turnout, Voting Preferences, and Political Involvement in Adulthood: The 1970 British Cohort Study." *Intelligence* 36, no. 6 (2008): 548–555.

Denny, Kevin, and Orla Doyle. "Political Interest, Cognitive Ability and Personality: Determinants of Voter Turnout in Britain." *British Journal of Political Science* 38, no. 2 (2008): 291–310.

Devine, Dennis J., and Jennifer L. Philips. "Do Smarter Teams Do Better? A Meta-Analysis of Cognitive Ability and Team Performance." *Small Group Research* 32, no. 5 (2001): 507–532.

Dodrill, Carl B. "Long-Term Reliability of the Wonderlic Personnel Test." *Journal of Consulting and Clinical Psychology* 51, no. 2 (1983): 316.

Dohmen, Thomas, Armin Falk, David Huffman, and Uwe Sunde. "Are Risk

Aversion and Impatience Related to Cognitive Ability?" *American Economic Review* 100, no. 3 (2010).

Drum, Kevin. "America's Real Criminal Element: Lead." *Mother Jones*, (January/February, 2013).

The Economist. "Mens Sana in Corpore Sano," July 2010.

Eppig, Christopher, Corey L. Fincher, and Randy Thornhill. "Parasite Prevalence and the Worldwide Distribution of Cognitive Ability." *Proceedings of the Royal Society B: Biological Sciences* 277, no. 1701 (2010): 3801–3808.

Farrar, Cynthia, Donald P. Green, Jennifer E. Green, David W. Nickerson, and Steven Shewfelt. "Does Discussion Group Composition Affect Policy Preferences? Results from Three Randomized Experiments." *Political Psychology* 30, no. 4 (2009): 615–647.

Ferraz, Claudio, and Frederico Finan. "Electoral Accountability and Corruption: Evidence from the Audits of Local Governments." National Bureau of Economic Research working paper, no. w14937 (2009).

Flore, Paulette C., and Jelte M. Wicherts. "Does Stereotype Threat Influence Performance of Girls in Stereotyped Domains? A Meta-Analysis." *Journal of School Psychology* 53, no. 1 (2015).

Flynn, James R. *Are We Getting Smarter? Rising IQ in the Twenty-First Century*. New York: Cambridge University Press, 2012.

———. "The 'Flynn Effect' and Flynn's Paradox." *Intelligence* 41, no. 6 (2013): 851–857.

———. "Massive IQ Gains in 14 Nations: What IQ Tests Really Measure." *Psychological Bulletin* 101, no. 2 (1987): 171.

———. *What Is Intelligence? Beyond the Flynn Effect*. New York: Cambridge University Press, 2007.

Gates, Bill. "Annual Letter from Bill Gates: 2011," Bill and Melinda Gates Foundation, January 2011.

Georgas, James, Fons van de Vijver, and Donald Saklofske. *Culture and Children's Intelligence: Cross-Cultural Analysis of the WISC-III*. Amsterdam: Elsevier, 2003.

Gillette, Clayton P. "Can Public Debt Enhance Democracy?" *William & Mary Law Review* 50, no. 3 (November, 2008).

Gorman, Linda. "The Impact of Childhood Lead Exposure on Adult Crime." *NBER Digest* (May, 2008).

Hamilton, Kirk, and Michael Clemens. "Genuine Savings Rates in Developing Countries." *The World Bank Economic Review* 13, no. 2 (1999): 333–356.

Hanushek, Erik A., and Dennis D. Kimko. "Schooling, Labor-Force Quality, and the Growth of Nations." *American Economic Review* 90, no 5 (2000): 1184–1208.

Hauser, Seth M. "Education, Ability, and Civic Engagement in the Contemporary United States." *Social Science Research* 29, no. 4 (2000): p. 556.

Hendricks, Lutz. "How Important Is Human Capital for Development? Evidence from Immigrant Earnings," *American Economic Review* 92, no. 1 (2002): 198–219.

Hochschild, Jennifer L. "If Democracies Need Informed Voters, How Can They Thrive While Expanding Enfranchisement?" *Election Law Journal* 9, no. 2 (2010): 111–123.

Hoxby, Caroline. "Peer Effects in the Classroom: Learning from Gender and Race Variation," National Bureau of Economic Research working paper no. 7867, 2000.

Hoyer, Wayne, Deborah J. MacInnis, and Rik Pieters. *Consumer Behavior*. Boston: Cengage Learning, 2012.

Hung, Juann H., and Rong Qian. "Why Is China's Saving Rate So High? A Comparative Study of Cross-Country Panel Data." Congressional Budget Office working paper, 2010.

Hunt, Earl B. *Human Intelligence*. New York: Cambridge University Press, 2011.

International Monetary Fund, "World Economic Outlook Database," October 2014 edition, http://www.imf.org/external/pubs/ft/weo/2014/02/weodata/weoselser.aspx, accessed February 15, 2015.

Iwawaki, Saburo, and Philip E. Vernon. "Japanese Abilities and Achievements." In *Human Abilities in Cultural Context*, ed. S. H. Irvine and J. W. Berry. New York: Cambridge University Press, 1988.

Jackson, Matthew O. *Social and Economic Networks*. Princeton, NJ: Princeton University Press, 2010.

Jefferson, Thomas. "Letter to Charles Yancey." In *The Works of Thomas Jefferson*, Federal Edition. New York and London: G.P. Putnam's Sons, 1904–1905, Vol. 11, p. 493.

Jensen, Arthur. *Bias in Mental Testing*. London: Methuen, 1980.

Jensen, Michael C. "Agency costs of free cash flow, corporate finance, and takeovers." *American Economic Review* 76, no. 2 (1986).

Jerven, Morten. *Poor Numbers: How We Are Misled by African Development Statistics and What to Do About It*. Ithaca: Cornell University Press, 2013.

Jones, Garett. "Are Smarter Groups More Cooperative? Evidence from Prisoner's Dilemma Experiments, 1959–2003." *Journal of Economic Behavior and Organization* 68, no. 3 (2008): 49–497.

———. "Are Smarter Groups More Cooperative? Results for Corrected and Extended Datasets." Working paper, George Mason University, 2013.

———. "The O-Ring Sector and the Foolproof Sector: An Explanation for Skill Externalities." *Journal of Economic Behavior & Organization* 85 (2013): 1–10.

———. "Will the Intelligent Inherit the Earth? IQ and Time Preference in the Global Economy." Working paper, George Mason University, 2012.

Jones, Garett, and Niklas Potrafke. "Human Capital and National Institutional Quality: Are TIMSS, PISA, and National Average IQ Robust Predictors?" *Intelligence* 46 (2014): 148–155.

Jones, Garett, and W. Joel Schneider. "Intelligence, Human Capital, and Economic Growth: A Bayesian Averaging of Classical Estimates (BACE) Approach." *Journal of Economic Growth* 11, no. 1 (2006): 71–93.

Jones, Garett, and W. Joel Schneider. "IQ in the Production Function: Evidence from Immigrant Earnings." *Economic Inquiry* 48, no. 3 (2010): 743–755.

Kahan, Dan M., Ellen Peters, Erica Cantrell Dawson, and Paul Slovic. "Motivated Numeracy and Enlightened Self-Government." Yale Law School, Public Law working paper, no. 307, 2013.

Kanazawa, Satoshi, and Linus Fontaine. "Intelligent People Defect More in a One-Shot Prisoner's Dilemma Game." *Journal of Neuroscience, Psychology, and Economics* 6, no. 3 (2013): 201.

Kanyama, Isaac Kalonda. "Quality of Institutions: Does Intelligence Matter?" *Intelligence* 42 (2014): 44–52.

Klein, Ezra. "How Politics Makes Us Stupid." *Vox.com*, April 6, 2014. http://www.vox.com/2014/4/6/5556462/brain-dead-how-politics-makes-us-stupid, accessed February 8, 2015.

Knight, Frank H. "Intellectual Confusion on Morals and Economics." *International Journal of Ethics* 45, no. 2 (January 1935): 200–220.

Kranzler, John H., and Arthur R. Jensen, "Inspection Time and Intelligence: A Meta-Analysis," *Intelligence* 13, no. 4 (1989): 329–347.

Kraus, Nancy, Torbjörn Malmfors, and Paul Slovic. "Intuitive Toxicology: Expert and Lay Judgments of Chemical Risks." *Risk Analysis* 12, no. 2 (1992): 215–232.

Kremer, Michael. "The O-Ring Theory of Economic Development." *Quarterly Journal of Economics* 108, no. 3 (1993): 551–575.

Kuhn, Peter, Peter Kooreman, Adriaan Soetevent, and Arie Kapteyn. "The Effects of Lottery Prizes on Winners and Their Neighbors: Evidence from the Dutch Postcode Lottery," *The American Economic Review* 101, no. 5 (2011): 2226–2247.

Kydland, Finn, and Edward C. Prescott. "Rules Rather Than Discretion: The Inconsistency of Optimal Plans." *Journal of Political Economy* (1977): 473–491.

Lane, Philip R., and Gian Maria Milesi-Ferretti, "The External Wealth of Nations Mark II: Revised and Extended Estimates of Foreign Assets and Liabilities, 1970–2004." *Journal of International Economics* 73, no. 2 (2007): 223–250.

Lynn, Richard, and Gerhard Meisenberg. "The Average IQ of Sub-Saharan Africans: Comments on Wicherts, Dolan, and van der Maas." *Intelligence* 38, no. 1 (2010): 21–29.

Lynn, Richard, and Gerhard Meisenberg. "National IQs Calculated and Validated for 108 Nations." *Intelligence* 38, no. 4 (2010): 353–360.

Lynn, Richard, and Tatu Vanhanen. *IQ and Global Inequality*. Whitefish, MT: Washington Summit, 2006.

Lynn, Richard, and Tatu Vanhanen. *IQ and the Wealth of Nations*. Santa Barbara, CA: Greenwood, 2002.

Mackintosh, Nicholas J. *IQ and Human Intelligence*, 2nd ed. Oxford: Oxford University Press, 2011.

Mas, Alexandre, and Enrico Moretti. "Peers at Work." *American Economic Review* 99, no. 1 (2009): 112–145.

McHenry, Jeffrey J., Leaetta M. Hough, Jody L. Toquam, Mary Ann Hanson, and Steven Ashworth. "Project A Validity Results: The Relationship Between Predictor and Criterion Domains." *Personnel Psychology* 43, no. 2 (1990): 335–354.

McNeil, Donald G. "In Raising the World's IQ, the Secret's in the Salt." *New York Times*, December 16, 2006.

Millet, Kobe, and Siegfried Dewitte. "Altruistic Behavior as a Costly Signal of General Intelligence." *Journal of Research in Personality* 41, no. 2 (2007): 316–326.

Moreale, Jennifer, and John Levendis. "IQ and Economic Development: A Critique of Lynn and Vanhanen." *Forum for Social Economics* 43, no. 1, (2014): 40–56.

Nevin, Rick. "Understanding International Crime Trends: The Legacy of Preschool Lead Exposure." *Environmental Research* 104, no. 3 (2007): 315–336.

Nickerson, David W. "Social Networks and Political Context." In *Cambridge Handbook of Experimental Political Science*, edited by J. N. Druckman, D. P. Green, J. H. Kuklinski, and A. Lupia. New York: Cambridge University Press, 2011.

Nisbett, Richard E. *Intelligence and How to Get It: Why Schools and Cultures Count*. New York: W.W. Norton, 2009.

Nisbett, Richard E., Joshua Aronson, Clancy Blair, William Dickens, James Flynn, Diane F. Halpern, and Eric Turkheimer. "Intelligence: New Findings and Theoretical Developments." *American Psychologist* 67, no. 2 (2012): 130–159.

Noelle-Neumann, Elisabeth. "The Spiral of Silence: A Theory of Public Opinion." *Journal of Communication* 24, no. 2 (1974): 43–51.

Nye, John V. C., and Charles C. Moul. "The Political Economy of Numbers: On the Application of Benford's Law to International Macroeconomic Statistics." *The BE Journal of Macroeconomics* 7, no. 1 (2007).

Oechssler, Jorg, Andreas Roider, and Patrick W. Schmitz. "Cognitive Abilities and Behavioral Biases." *Journal of Economic Behavior & Organization* 72, no. 1 (2009): 147–152.

Ordeshook, Peter C. *Game Theory and Political Theory: An Introduction*. New York: Cambridge University Press, 1986: 240.

Ottaviano, Gianmarco I. P., and Giovanni Peri. "Rethinking the Effect of Immigration on Wages." *Journal of the European Economic Association* 10, no. 1 (2012): 152–197.

Pande, Rohini. "Can Informed Voters Enforce Better Governance? Experiments in Low-Income Democracies." *Annual Review of Economics* 3, no. 1 (2011): 215–237.

Potrafke, Niklas. "Intelligence and Corruption." *Economics Letters* 114, no. 1 (2012): 109–112.

Proto, Eugenio, Aldo Rustichini, and Andis Sofianos. "Higher Intelligence Groups Have Higher Cooperation Rates in the Repeated Prisoner's Dilemma." IZA discussion paper no. 8499, 2014.

Putterman, Louis, Jean-Robert Tyran, and Kenju Kamei. "Public Goods and Voting on Formal Sanction Schemes." *Journal of Public Economics* 95, no. 9 (2011): 1213–1222.

Ram, Rati. "IQ and Economic Growth: Further Augmentation of Mankiw-Romer-Weil Model." *Economics Letters* 94, no. 1 (2007): 7–11.

Ramsey, Frank P. "A Mathematical Theory of Saving." *The Economic Journal* (1928): 543–559.

Raven Matrix. *User: Life of Riley*. Licensed under Creative Commons Attribution-Share Alike 3.0 via Wikimedia Commons in Wikipedia. http://commons.wikimedia.org/wiki/File:Raven_Matrix.svg#mediaviewer/File:Raven_Matrix.svg.

Reyes, Jessica Wolpaw. "Environmental Policy as Social Policy? The Impact of Childhood Lead Exposure on Crime." *The BE Journal of Economic Analysis & Policy* 7, no. 1 (2007).

Rindermann, Heiner. "The g-Factor of International Cognitive Ability Comparisons: The Homogeneity of Results in PISA, TIMSS, PIRLS and IQ-Tests Across Nations." *European Journal of Personality* 21 no. 5 (2007): 667–706.

Rindermann, Heiner, Carmen Flores-Mendoza, and Michael A. Woodley. "Political Orientations, Intelligence and Education." *Intelligence* 40, no. 2 (2012): 217–225.

Rindermann, Heiner, Michael Sailer, and James Thompson. "The Impact of Smart Fractions, Cognitive Ability of Politicians and Average Competence of Peoples on Social Development." *Talent Development & Excellence* 1, no. 1 (2009): 3–25.

Rindermann, Heiner, and James Thompson. "Cognitive Capitalism: The Effect of Cognitive Ability on Wealth, as Mediated Through Scientific Achievement and Economic Freedom." *Psychological Science* 22, no. 6 (2011): 754–763.

Roberts, Russ. "If You're Paying, I'll Have Top Sirloin." *Wall Street Journal*, May 18, 1995.

Rutter, Owen (ed.). *The History of the Seventh (Service) Battalion, The Royal Sussex Regiment, 1914–1919*. London: The Times Publishing Company, 1934.

Schmidt, Frank L., and John E. Hunter. "The Validity and Utility of Selection Methods in Personnel Psychology: Practical and Theoretical Implications of 85 Years of Research Findings." *Psychological Bulletin* 124, no. 2 (1998): 262–274.

Schoon, Ingrid, Helen Cheng, Catharine R. Gale, G. David Batty, and Ian J. Deary. "Social Status, Cognitive Ability, and Educational Attainment as Predictors of Liberal Social Attitudes and Political Trust." *Intelligence* 38, no. 1 (2010): 144–150.

Seabright, Paul. *The Company of Strangers*. Princeton, NJ: Princeton University Press, 2004.

Segal, Nancy L., and Scott L. Hershberger. "Cooperation and Competition Between Twins: Findings from a Prisoner's Dilemma Game." *Evolution and Human Behavior* 20, no. 1 (1999): 29–51.

Shamosh, Noah A., and Jeremy R. Gray. "Delay Discounting and Intelligence: A Meta-Analysis." *Intelligence* 36, no. 4 (2008): 289–305.

Sharma, Sudeep, William Bottom, and Hillary Anger Elfenbein. "On the Role of Personality, Cognitive Ability, and Emotional Intelligence in Predicting Negotiation Outcomes: A Meta-Analysis." *Organizational Psychology Review* 3, no. 4 (2013): 293–336.

Solon, Orville, Travis J. Riddell, Stella A. Quimbo, Elizabeth Butrick, Glen P. Aylward, Marife Lou Bacate, and John W. Peabody. "Associations Between Cognitive Function, Blood Lead Concentration, and Nutrition Among Children in the Central Philippines." *The Journal of Pediatrics* 152, no. 2 (2008): 237–243.

Spearman, Charles. "'General Intelligence,' Objectively Determined and Measured." *The American Journal of Psychology* 15, no. 2 (1904): 201–292.

Stanovich, Keith E., Anne E. Cunningham, and Dorothy J. Freeman. "Intelligence, Cognitive Skills, and Early Reading Progress." *Reading Research Quarterly* 19, no. 3 (1984): 278–303.

Strenze, Tarmo. "Intelligence and Socioeconomic Success: A Meta-Analytic Review of Longitudinal Research." *Intelligence* 35, no. 5 (2007): 401–426.

Tabarrok, Alexander T., and David J. Theroux. "Open Letter on Immigration." *The Independent Institute*, June 19, 2006. http://www.independent.org/newsroom/article.asp?id=1727, accessed February 8, 2015.

Terhune, Kenneth W. "'Wash-In,' 'Wash-Out,' and Systemic Effects in Extended Prisoner's Dilemma." *Journal of Conflict Resolution* 18, no. 4 (December 1974): 656–685.

United Nations Environmental Program. "Sub-Saharan Africa Lead Matrix," last updated March 2010, http://www.unep.org/transport/pcfv/PDF/MatrixAfricaLead-March2010.pdf.

Warner, John T., and Saul Pleeter. "The Personal Discount Rate: Evidence from Military Downsizing Programs." *American Economic Review* 91, no. 1 (2001): 33–53.

Weede, Erich, and Sebastian Kämpf. "The Impact of Intelligence and Institutional Improvements on Economic Growth." *Kyklos* 55, no. 3 (2002): 361–380.

Weinberg, Warren A., Susan G. Dietz, Elizabeth C. Penick, and William H. McAlister. "Intelligence, Reading Achievement, Physical Size, and Social Class: A Study of St. Louis Caucasian Boys Aged 8-0 to 9-6 Years, Attending Regular Schools," *Journal of Pediatrics* 85, no. 4 (1974): 482–489.

Wicherts, Jelte M., Conor V. Dolan, Jerry S. Carlson, and Han L. J. van der Maas. "Another Failure to Replicate Lynn's Estimate of the Average IQ of Sub-Saharan Africans." *Learning and Individual Differences* 20, no. 3 (2010): 155–157.

Wicherts, Jelte M., Conor V. Dolan, Jerry S. Carlson, and Han L. J. van der Maas. "Raven's Test Performance of Sub-Saharan Africans: Average Performance, Psychometric Properties, and the Flynn Effect." *Learning and Individual Differences* 20, no. 3 (2010): 135–151.

Wicherts, Jelte M., Conor V. Dolan, and Han L. J. van der Maas. "The Dangers of Unsystematic Selection Methods and the Representativeness of 46 samples of African Test-Takers." *Intelligence* 38, no. 1 (2010): 30–37.

Wicherts, Jelte M., Conor V. Dolan, and Han L. J. van der Maas. "A Systematic Literature Review of the Average IQ of Sub-Saharan Africans." *Intelligence* 38, no. 1 (2010): 1–20.

Williams, Robert L. "Overview of the Flynn Effect." *Intelligence* 41, no. 6 (2013): 753–764.

Wittman, Donald A. *The Myth of Democratic Failure: Why Political Institutions Are Efficient.* Chicago: University of Chicago Press, 1995.

Wolfinger, Raymond E., and Steven J. Rosenstone. *Who Votes?* New Haven: Yale University Press, 1980.

Woolley, Anita Williams, Christopher F. Chabris, Alex Pentland, Nada Hashmi, and Thomas W. Malone. "Evidence for a Collective Intelligence Factor in the Performance of Human Groups." *Science* 330, no. 6004 (2010): 686–688.

Young, Alwyn. "The African Growth Miracle." *Journal of Political Economy* 120, no. 4 (2012): 696–739.

Zax, Jeffrey S., and Daniel I. Rees. "IQ, Academic Performance, Environment, and Earnings." *Review of Economics and Statistics* 84, no. 4 (2002): 600–616.

INDEX

abstract thinking and IQ tests, 51–52, 58–59, 62
Acemoglu, Daron, 111–13
Alderman, Harold, 174n12
al-Ubaydli, Omar, 98–99
Argentina: average cognitive ability score in, 169; average IQ score in, 72, 117, 169; savings rate in, 72
Armenia: average cognitive ability score in, 169; average IQ score in, 169
Arrow, Kenneth: on economic backwardness and lack of mutual confidence, 113
Asch, Solomon: on opinions and social conformity, 131–34, 136, 167; "Opinions and Social Pressure", 131, 132
Atlas Shrugged: Francisco d'Anconia in, 114
Australia: average cognitive ability score in, 169; average IQ score in, 169; IQ-income relationship in, 32
Austria: average cognitive ability score in, 169; average IQ score in, 169
Axelrod, Robert: on cooperation, 85, 89–91, 96, 103–4, 167; *The Evolution of Cooperation*, 85, 89–90, 103–4; on patience, 91; on repeated prisoner's dilemmas (RPDs), 89–91, 103–5; on shadow of the future, 91, 99, 104; on tit for tat strategy, 103–4, 176n4; on unwritten WWI peace treaties, 103–5

Bahrain: average cognitive ability score in, 169; average IQ score in, 117, 169
Barro, Robert: *Economic Growth*, 76–79, 130; on international capital flows, 77–79; on patience, 77–79; on reputation, 115–16
behavioral economics, 66–68
Behrman, Jere R., 174n12
Belgium: average cognitive ability score in, 169; average IQ score in, 169
Bell Telephone System, 28–29
Benjamin, Daniel J., 67–68
Bils, Mark, 171n7
Borjas, George, 159, 160
Bosnia: average cognitive ability score in, 169; average IQ score in, 169
Botswana: average cognitive ability score in, 169; average IQ score in, 169
Bowles, Samuel, 31–32, 99

brain, the: brain scans and hyperbolic discounting, 67; brain scans and IQ, 13, 24–26; as computer, 25–26; health of, 54; limbic system, 67; prefrontal cortex, 67; size of, 24–26, 27, 28, 55

Brazil: average cognitive ability score in, 9, 169; average IQ score in, 47, 72, 169; da Vinci Effect in, 47; GDP per person and cognitive ability in, 9; government audits in, 130; informed voters in, 130; political attitudes and IQ in, 129; savings rate in, 72

Brennan, Jason: on epistocracy, 136–37

British Columbia, 44

Brown, Sebastian A., 67–68

Buchanan, James: on imposing order on chaos, 109; on limited time-span of decision-makers, 111; *The Limits of Liberty*, 109, 111

Bulgaria: average cognitive ability score in, 169; average IQ score in, 169

Burke, Mary A., 60

Canada: average cognitive ability score in, 169; average IQ score in, 72, 117, 169; British Columbia, 44; IQ-income relationship in, 32

Caplan, Bryan: on conformity, 73; on immigrants and politics, 162–63; on informed voters, 123–25, 130, 161, 167; on irrational voters, 121; *The Myth of the Rational Voter*, 121, 123; on pro-market attitudes, 124–25, 129

CEOs, 83

Cesarini, David, 94–95

Chabris, Christopher, 146–47

cheap talk, 147, 149–51

Chile, 67; average cognitive ability score in, 169; average IQ score in, 72, 117

China: average IQ in, 72, 117; average national test scores in, 2, 7, 45, 72; economic conditions in, 2, 45; as lender to U.S., 82; political conditions in, 2; savings rate in, 72, 80

Christiakis, Nicholas: *Connected*, 59–60

Coase, Ronald/Coase Theorem, 106–13, 118, 166

Cobb-Douglas production function, 153–58

cognitive ability, 2, 10; cross-country comparisons regarding, 7–9, 169, 170, 171n5; of elites, 28–29, 165–66; and human relationships, 147–48; Rindermann on, 7–9, 46, 47, 166, 170, 171n5; skill in one area predicting skill in another, 15–16, 18–20, 22, 23, 28–29, 44, 46–47, 68, 70, 123, 167. *See also* da Vinci effect

Cognitive Reflection Test, 68

collective intelligence/hive mind: defined, 12; poetic summary, 165

Colombia: average cognitive ability score in, 169; average IQ score in, 169

colonialism, 14, 118

common interests, 149–51

common sense, 101–2, 116

computer speed, 17–18, 172n1

conformity, 13, 73–74, 131–36, 162–63, 167

Congressional Budget Office, 80

consumer spending, 73–74

cooperation: Axelrod on, 85, 89–91, 96, 103–4, 167; conditional cooperators, 98–99, 177n13; and conformity, 13; difficulty of, 85–86; relationship to IQ scores, 1, 13, 84, 86, 91–92, 96–102, 150–51; relationship to patience, 91, 92, 96, 110; relationship to pleasantness/generosity, 91, 92–94, 96, 99, 110; relationship to prosperity, 105; relationship to SAT scores, 96–97; relationship to social perceptiveness, 91–92, 96, 110; and repeated prisoner's dilemmas (RPDs), 88–94, 96–100; and self-interest, 85–87, 89; and tit for tat strategy, 89, 90–91, 98–99, 176n4; and trust, 88–89, 91, 92–93
corporate downsizing, 124
Corruption Perceptions Index, 117
Covey, Steven: on pie-growing vs. pie-grabbing, 2–3; on success, 2–3; on "Think Win-Win" habit, 2–3
Cowen, Tyler: on immigration and good politics, 161
Cowgill, Bo, 134–35
Crawford, Vincent: on theory of cheap talk, 147, 149–51
Croatia: average cognitive ability score in, 169; average IQ score in, 169
cross-country comparisons, 35–48, 50; regarding cognitive ability, 7–9, 169, 170, 171n5; regarding da Vinci Effect, 46–47; regarding education, 122; regarding GDP, 8–9, 10–11, 13–14, 171n5; regarding government corruption, 1–2, 117; regarding IQ scores, 38–44, 46, 48, 117–18, 169, 170; regarding productivity, 7–9, 139–41; regarding savings, 72–73, 80–81; source of IQ scores for, 38–44, 46, 48, 170; regarding standardized test scores, 1–2, 7–9, 10–11, 13–14, 171n5
crystallized intelligence, 58
culture, 14, 36–37, 52, 80
Culture and Children's Intelligence, 39
Czech Republic: average cognitive ability score in, 169; average IQ score in, 169

da Vinci Effect: and computer speed, 17–18, 172n1; cross-country comparisons regarding, 46–47; defined, 15–16, 22, 44; and emotional/social intelligence, 33–34; regarding IQ and cognitive ability, 15–16, 18–20, 22, 23, 28–29, 44, 46–47, 68, 70, 123, 167; and Raven's matrices, 23; and Spearman, 18–20; regarding strength, 18, 172n1; regarding teams, 146–47; and wages, 44
Davis, Steven J., 144
debt, corporate, 82–83
debt, international, 77, 78, 81–84; default on, 81, 82
democracy: accountability of politicians, 130–31; and Coase Theorem, 108; informed voters, 122–31, 136–37, 162, 165, 167. *See also* politics
Denmark: average cognitive ability score in, 169; average IQ score in, 169; education in, 122
Devine, Dennis, 146
division of labor, 151–52, 159–60
Dohmen, Thomas, 65–66

Dreary, Ian, 26
Drum, Kevin, 63

East Asia: average IQ scores in, 42, 43, 44–46, 50, 64, 80–81, 168; math test scores in, 35, 45; savings rates in, 80
economic conditions: in China, 2, 45; in Finland, 1–2; in Hong Kong, 45; property rights, 105–6, 117, 118, 166; relationship to national average IQ, 1–2, 5, 11–12, 13–14, 34, 35–36, 39, 40, 43–44, 55, 56, 57, 105–6, 124–26, 154, 167–68, 171n7; relationship to standardized test scores, 1–2, 5–9, 10–12, 34, 35, 39, 40, 43–44, 55, 166; in Singapore, 1–2, 8; in Taiwan, 45; voter information and national prosperity, 137
Economist, The, 38
education: and abstract thinking, 58–59; informed voters, 122–31, 136–37, 162, 165, 167; and peer effect, 59–60; relationship to intelligence, 57–59; relationship to IQ scores, 31, 32, 41, 42, 43, 50, 56, 57–59, 60, 65–66, 119, 128, 167, 168; relationship to national prosperity, 5–6, 50, 56, 124–26, 171n7; relationship to wages, 30, 48; as saving for the future, 73; standardized test scores vs. years of, 5–7
Egypt: average cognitive ability score in, 9, 169; average IQ score in, 169; GDP per person and cognitive ability in, 9
elementary cognitive tasks (ECTs), 27
emotional intelligence, 32–34, 147

endogenous network formation and IQ scores, 147–48
Enlightenment liberalism, 129
epistocracy, 136–37, 162
Estonia: average cognitive ability score in, 169; average IQ score in, 169
exceptions, 4, 8, 9, 16, 17, 22–23, 24, 33, 165

Falk, Armin, 65–66
family background, 42–43, 49, 61, 65–66, 67, 68
Feldstein-Horioka puzzle, 75–76
Ferraz, Claudio, 130
financial markets, 75
Finan, Frederico, 130
Finland: average cognitive ability score in, 169; average IQ score in, 169; average national test scores in, 1–2; economic conditions in, 1–2; education in, 122; political conditions in, 1
Flore, Paulette C., 173n1
Flores-Mendoza, Carmen, 129
fluid intelligence, 57, 58–59
Flynn, James: on abstract thinking and IQ tests, 51–52, 58–59, 62; on academic freedom, 52; on economic equality, 52–53; Flynn Effect, 12, 51, 51–53, 60–64, 167–68, 175n18; on Ice Ages hypothesis, 53; on IQ gaps across demographic groups, 52–53; on Jensen, 52; "Massive IQ Gains in 14 Nations", 51; on value of IQ research, 52; on verbal similarities questions, 51–52
folk theorem, 89
Foolproof sector of economy, 153–58
Fowler, James: *Connected*, 59–60

France: average cognitive ability score in, 169; average IQ score in, 169; average national test scores in, 7
Frank, Robert: on consumer spending, 74
free riding, 109
free trade policies, 124, 125

game theory, 89, 99–100, 106
Gates, Bill: on IQ scores and disease, 38
GDP per person, 7–9, 10–11, 19, 170, 171n5
Gekko, Gordon: on greed, 86
gender equality, 129
general factor of intelligence. *See* da Vinci Effect
General Management Admissions Test (GMAT), 3–4
General Social Survey, 125
generosity/pleasantness, 91, 92–94, 96, 99, 110
genetic differences and IQ scores, 53
geography, 14
George Washington Social Intelligence Test, 33
Germany: average cognitive ability score in, 169; average IQ score in, 169
g factor. *See* da Vinci Effect
Ghana: average cognitive ability score in, 9, 169; average IQ score in, 169; GDP per person and cognitive ability in, 9
Gintis, Herbert, 31–32, 99
global financial crisis, 75
globalization, 79, 157
GMAT. *See* General Management Admissions Test
Google prediction markets, 134–35

Gordon, Robert: on reputation, 115–16
Gray, Jeremy R., 66, 69–70
Greece: average cognitive ability score in, 169; average IQ score in, 47, 169; da Vinci Effect in, 47
greed, 86–87, 106
GRE scores, 100
grocery checkout clerks, 144–45
Guatemala: malnutrition and IQ in, 56
gun control and crime, 126–27

haggling skills, 3
Haltiwanger, John, 144
Hanson, Robin, 134
Hanushek, Eric, 5–7
Hawaii, 44
health and IQ scores, 1, 38, 41, 42–43, 52, 54–56, 60, 119, 167, 168; lead abatement, 49–50, 62–64. *See also* nutrition and IQ scores
height: of identical twins, 22; relationship to gender, 23; relationship to IQ scores, 23–24, 25, 35
Heinlein, Robert, 91–92
Hendricks, Lutz, 47, 48, 174n17
Herrnstein, Richard: *The Bell Curve*, 51; on *Flynn Effect*, 51
Hobbes, Thomas, 106
Hochschild, Jennifer: on democratization, 136
Hoddinott, John, 174n12
home country bias, 79
homo economicus, 66, 67, 68
Hong Kong: average cognitive ability score in, 169; average IQ score in, 45, 169; da Vinci Effect in, 47; economic conditions in, 45; reading test scores in, 45; savings rate in, 72, 80

Hoxby, Caroline, 59
Huffman, David, 65–66
human capital, 56, 76, 118, 148, 162, 163
Hungary: average cognitive ability score in, 169; average IQ score in, 169
Hung, Juann H., on East Asian savings rates, 80
Hunt, Earl B., 25, 45–46; *Human Intelligence*, 173n1
Hunter, John, 28
hyperbolic discounting defined, 67

Ice Age hypothesis, 53
Iceland: average cognitive ability score in, 169; average IQ score in, 169
identical twins: body mass index (BMI) of, 22; height of, 22
imagination, 70–71
immigration, 152, 156–63, 174n17; relationship to politics, 161–63; relationship to wages, 47–48, 157–60; to United States, 47–48, 159–60, 174n17
Imperial, 81–82
impulsive behavior, 66–68
Independent Institute, 161
India: average IQ in, 72; savings rate in, 72
Indonesia: average cognitive ability score in, 169; average IQ score in, 169
indoor lighting, 62
infant birth weight and low IQ, 54–55
inflation temptation, 114
inspection time studies, 26–28
intelligence: as ability to recall difference types of information, 16; as ability to solve a variety of problems, 16; as ability to use deductive reasoning, 16; crystallized intelligence, 58, 62; fluid intelligence, 57, 58–59, 62; Machiavellian intelligence, 101–2, 118; relationship to brain size, 24–26, 27; relationship to education, 57–59; social intelligence, 32–34, 92, 148, 149, 152. *See also* da Vinci Effect
interest rates, 77–78, 81
international capital flows, 75–76, 77–84
International Monetary Fund (IMF), 175n8
investment: international investment, 71, 74–76, 77–84; relationship to productivity, 13, 76; relationship to savings, 13, 71–72, 74–76, 77–81; relationship to taxation, 116
iodine deficiency, 60–61
IQ tests: abstraction in, 51–52, 58–59, 62; bias in, 10, 21, 25–26, 36, 39, 43; as cognitive skill tests, 10; comprehensiveness of, 20–21; controversy regarding, 16, 19–20, 25–26; multiple choice tests as, 20–21, 61; vs. personality tests, 28–29; prevalence of, 10; Raven's Progressive Matrices, 20–21, 23, 27, 33, 35–36, 39, 40, 44, 51, 57, 58, 61, 92, 99, 129; and reverse digit span, 57, 70; Stanford-Binet IQ test, 15; verbal tests as, 23; visual-spatial tests as, 10, 20–21, 23, 33, 45; Wechsler IQ test, 15, 20, 37, 39, 51; Wonderlic IQ test, 176n10

IQ test scores: cross-country comparisons regarding, 38–44, 46, 48, 117–18, 169, 170; relationship to better-informed citizens, 1, 13; relationship to brain size, 25; relationship to building productive networks, 147–48; relationship to cheap talk, 149–51; relationship to cooperation, 1, 13, 84, 86, 91–92, 96–102, 150–51; relationship to education, 31, 32, 41, 42, 43, 56, 57–59, 65–66, 119, 128, 167, 168; relationship to emotional intelligence, 32–34, 147; relationship to generosity/pleasantness, 91, 92–94, 96, 99; relationship to government quality, 116–18, 129–31, 162; relationship to handling complexity, 3–4; relationship to health, 1, 38, 41, 42–43, 49–50, 52, 54–57, 60, 62–64, 119, 167, 168; relationship to inspection time, 26–27; relationship to job performance, 28–31; relationship to memory, 1, 13, 33, 44, 129, 147–48, 149; relationship to nutrition, 13, 35, 41, 42–43, 50, 52, 54–56, 59, 60–61, 119, 168; relationship to openness to new things, 101; relationship to patience, 1, 65–66, 67–73, 80–81, 84, 91, 92, 96; relationship to peer effects, 59–60, 146–47; relationship to pie-growing approach, 3–4, 100, 101; relationship to political attitudes, 127–29; relationship to poverty, 1, 9, 43, 45, 56–57; relationship to probability of voting, 127–28; relationship to pro-market attitudes, 13, 83–84, 124–26, 127, 129; relationship to reaction time, 27–28; relationship to reciprocation, 93; relationship to savings rate, 13, 68, 71–73; relationship to social intelligence, 32–34, 92, 94–96, 148, 149; relationship to social perceptiveness, 91–92, 94–96; relationship to successful use of technology, 13; relationship to success in life, 4–5, 6–7; relationship to wages, 4–5, 6–7, 14, 30–32, 35, 36, 43–44, 47–48, 49, 152, 153–54, 174n12; scores in one area predicting scores in other areas, 15–16, 18–20, 22, 23, 28–29, 44, 46–47, 68, 70, 123, 167; top 10 percent vs. bottom 10 percent regarding income, 31; variation over time, 22–23; visual-spatial scores vs. verbal scores, 23. *See also* national average IQ

IQ test scores, raising of, 10, 11–12, 38, 41, 43, 49–64, 163; Flynn Effect, 12, 51–53, 60–64, 167–68, 175n18; government policies regarding, 5, 50, 56, 58–59, 60, 62–64, 167; by improving education, 50, 58–59, 60, 167, 168; by improving health, 49–50, 50, 52, 54–56, 60, 62–64, 119, 167, 168; by improving nutrition, 41, 50, 52, 54–56, 60–61, 119, 168; by lead abatement, 49–50, 62–64

Iran: average cognitive ability score in, 169; average IQ score in, 117, 169; da Vinci Effect in, 47

Ireland: average cognitive ability score in, 169; average IQ score in, 169

Israel, 58; average cognitive ability score in, 169; average IQ score in, 47, 169; da Vinci Effect in, 47

Italy: average cognitive ability score in, 9, 169; average IQ score in, 169; GDP per person and cognitive ability in, 9

Jackson, Matthew: on theory of endogenous network formation, 147–48
Japan: average cognitive ability score in, 169; average IQ score in, 39, 45, 72, 117, 169; GDP per person and cognitive ability in, 9; reading test scores in, 45; rising IQ scores in, 50; savings rate in, 80
Jefferson, Thomas: on freedom and ignorance, 136, 137
Jensen, Arthur: *Bias in Mental Testing*, 173n1; on IQ differences across demographic groups, 52
Jensen, Michael C., 83
Jerven, Morten: *Poor Numbers*, 170
job interviews, 24, 28
job performance, 13, 28–31, 34
Jordan: average cognitive ability score in, 169; average IQ score in, 169

Kahan, Dan, 126–27
Kämpf, Sebastian, 171n7
Kanyama, Isaac Kalonda, 118
Katz, Larry, 159
Kenya: average IQ score in, 72, 117; savings rate in, 72
Keynesian Beauty Contest, 95–96
Keynes, John Maynard, 66, 95–96
Kimko, Dennis, 5–7
Klein, Ezra, 127
Klenow, Peter J., 171n7
Knight, Frank: on social order and cheating, 103
Kraus, Nancy, 121–22, 124

Kremer, Michael: on O-ring theory of productivity, 139–41, 153, 167
Kuhn, Peter, 74
Kuwait: average cognitive ability score in, 169; average IQ score in, 169
Kydland, Finn: on time inconsistency in government planning, 114–15

Lane, Philip, 79
law of one price (LOOP), 155–56, 157, 158
lead exposure and IQ, 49–50, 62–64
Lebanon: average cognitive ability score in, 169; average IQ score in, 169
legal systems, 105–6, 115
Levendis, John, 171n7
literacy test scores, 1, 6, 7–9, 46
Lithuania: average cognitive ability score in, 169; average IQ score in, 169
long time horizons, 104–5
lottery winners, 74
Luxembourg: GDP per person and cognitive ability in, 9
Lynn, Richard: on average IQ scores in Sub-Saharan Africa, 41–44, 56; dataset of, 38–44, 46, 48; and Flynn, 51; *IQ and the Wealth of Nations*, 38, 40–41; national average IQ estimates of, 46, 48, 170; on rising IQ scores in Japan, 50; Weicherts on, 41–44, 56

Machiavellian intelligence, 100–102, 118
Mackintosh, N. J., 34, 54
macroeconomics, 66, 71–72
Malaysia: average cognitive ability

score in, 169; average IQ score in, 169
Malta: average cognitive ability score in, 169; average IQ score in, 169
market-oriented attitudes: and informed voters, 137; and IQ scores, 13, 83–84, 124–26, 127, 129
Marx, Karl: on alienation, 152
Mas, Alexandre, 145
maternal alcohol abuse and IQ, 54
maternal breast-feeding and IQ, 55
maternal exercise and IQ, 55
maternal nutrition and IQ, 54–55
math test scores, 1, 5–9, 10, 37, 40, 46, 117, 126–27, 167, 173n1; in East Asia, 35, 45
McCabe, Kevin, 92, 101
Meckling, William H., 83
Meisenberg, Gerhard, 170
memory, 70, 151, 152; and accountability of politicians, 129–30; relationship to IQ scores, 1, 13, 33, 44, 129, 147–48, 149
Mexico: average cognitive ability score in, 9, 169; average IQ score in, 47, 169; da Vinci Effect in, 47; GDP per person and cognitive ability in, 9
Milesi-Ferretti, Gian Maria, 79
Miller, Stephen, 125, 129
Montenegro: average IQ score in, 117
Moreale, Jennifer, 171n7
Moretti, Enrico, 144
Morocco: average cognitive ability score in, 169; average IQ score in, 47, 169; da Vinci Effect in, 47
moviemaking, 142
MRI and IQ, 24–26, 27
MSCEIT (Mayer-Salovey-Caruso Emotional Intelligence Test), 33–34

Mullainathan, Sendil: on poverty and IQ scores, 56–57; *Scarcity*, 56–57
multinational corporations, 75–76
multiple regression, 11, 79, 117, 124
multiplier effect, 7, 131, 148, 168
Murray, Charles: *The Bell Curve*, 51; on *Flynn Effect*, 51

national average IQ: cross-country comparisons, 38–44, 46, 48, 117–18, 169, 170; vs. individual IQ, 4–5, 6–7, 167; policies regarding, 5, 56, 58–59, 60, 62–64, 167; relationship to foreign investment, 79, 84; relationship to government corruption, 117, 162; relationship to government quality, 116–18, 129–31, 162; relationship to IQ of politicians, 118–19, 125; relationship to national prosperity and productivity, 1–2, 5, 11–12, 13–14, 34, 35–36, 39, 40, 43–44, 55, 56, 57, 105–6, 124–26, 154, 167–68, 171n7; relationship to savings, 72–73, 76, 84; scores in East Asia, 42, 43, 44–46, 50, 64, 80–81, 168
natural resources, 2, 9, 72–73, 111
negotiation: negotiation games, 100, 116; negotiation skills, 3–4, 106–10; win-win outcomes, 106–8, 109–10, 113, 151
Netherlands: average cognitive ability score in, 169; average IQ score in, 72, 169; famine during WWII, 54–55; lotteries in, 74; savings rate in, 72
New Zealand: Alliance party, 53; average cognitive ability score in, 169; average IQ score in, 169; IQ-income relationship in, 32

Nickerson, David, 132
Nisbett, Richard E., 173n1; *Intelligence and How to Get It*, 55
Noelle-Neumann, Elisabeth: on spiral of silence, 132
Norway: average cognitive ability score in, 9, 169; average IQ score in, 40, 169; GDP per person and cognitive ability in, 9
nutrition and IQ scores, 13, 35, 41, 42–43, 50, 52, 54–56, 59, 60–61, 119, 168. *See also* health and IQ scores

Obama, Barack, 82
Oman: average cognitive ability score in, 169; average IQ score in, 169
one-shot games, 89, 100–101, 104, 109
Ordeshook, Peter: *Game Theory and Political Theory*, 104; on prisoner's dilemma and government inefficiency, 104
O-ring theory of production, 139–47, 152, 153–58
Osborne, Melissa, 31–32
Ottaviano, Gianmarco I. P., 159–60

Pakistan: income-IQ relationship in, 44
Palestine: average cognitive ability score in, 169; average IQ score in, 169
Pande, Rohini, 129–30
paradox of IQ, 32; defined, 5, 6–7, 167
patience: Barro and Sala-i-Martin on, 77–79; and conformity, 13; in politics, 105, 111–16; Ramsey on, 71, 167; relationship to cooperation, 91, 92, 96, 110; relationship to IQ scores, 1, 65–66, 67–73, 80–81, 84, 91, 92, 96; and savings, 71–73, 74, 75, 77–79, 84; as virtue, 76–81
peer effects, 152; and IQ scores, 59–60, 146–47
perceptiveness, social: and IQ, 91–92, 94–96; relationship to cooperation, 91–92, 96, 110
Peri, Giovanni, 159–60
personality tests, 28–29, 151
Philippines: average cognitive ability score in, 9, 169; average IQ score in, 169; GDP per person and cognitive ability in, 9; lead exposure in, 49–50
Philips, Jennifer, 146
pie-growing, 108, 112; relationship to IQ scores, 3–4, 100, 101; vs. pie-grabbing approach, 2–4
PIRLS (Progress in International Reading Literacy Study), 6, 7–9, 46, 47, 170
PISA (Programme for International Student Assessment), 6, 7–9, 10, 45, 46, 47, 166, 170
Pleeter, Saul, 69
Poland: average cognitive ability score in, 169; average IQ score in, 47, 169; da Vinci Effect in, 47
politics: accountability of politicians, 130–31; and Coase Theorem, 108–9, 110, 111–13, 118, 166; corruption in, 1, 2, 84, 110–11, 117, 130, 162; epistocracy, 136–37, 162; government policies regarding IQ scores, 5, 50, 56, 58–59, 60, 62–64, 167; government promises, 114–16; government quality and IQ scores, 116–18, 129–31, 162; infla-

tion temptation, 114–15; informed voters, 122–31, 136–37, 162, 165, 167; IQ scores of politicians, 118–19, 125; and long time horizons, 104–5; patience in, 105, 111–16; political attitudes and IQ scores, 127–29; political attitudes and social conformity, 132–34; political regimes, 105–6; prosperity and cooperation in, 105; relationship to immigration, 161–63; relationship to national standardized test scores, 1, 2; repeated prisoner's dilemmas (RPDs) in, 105–6; and self-interest, 87; speech of politicians, 150; time inconsistency in government planning, 114–15

Portugal: average cognitive ability score in, 169; average IQ score in, 169

Potrafke, Niklas, 117, 166

poverty: and immigration, 161; and IQ scores, 1, 9, 43, 45, 56–57

Prescott, Ed: on time inconsistency in government planning, 114–15

prisoner's dilemma, 86–94, 113, 116; as one-shot game, 89, 100–101, 104, 109; repeated prisoner's dilemmas (RPDs), 88–94, 96–100, 103–6, 110, 176nn4,10

productivity: as GDP per person, 7–9, 19; O-ring theory of, 139–47, 152, 153; relationship to cognitive skill levels, 165–66; relationship to division of labor, 151–52; relationship to education, 30–31; relationship to imitation, 144–46; relationship to IQ scores, 1, 2, 5, 8–9, 11, 12, 13, 34, 35–36, 40, 43, 57, 96, 146–47, 149, 152, 167–68;

relationship to savings rate, 13, 76; relationship to wages, 30–31, 140–41, 144, 156

pro-market attitudes and IQ scores, 13, 83–84, 124–26, 127, 129

property rights, 105–6, 117, 118, 166

psychological testing firms, 39–40

public goods game, 94

public opinion: regarding economic policies, 123–26; vs. expert opinion, 121–22, 123–24; relationship to social conformity, 131–36; role of education in, 122–29; regarding toxicology, 121–22, 124

Putterman, Louis, 94

Qatar: average cognitive ability score in, 9, 169; average IQ score in, 169; GDP per person and cognitive ability in, 9

Qian, Rong: on East Asian savings rates, 80

Quimbo, Stella, 49

racism, 129

Ramsey, Frank: on imagination, 71; on mathematical theory of saving, 71–72, 84; on patience, 71, 167; Ramsey growth model, 71; on saving and investment, 71–72, 74, 77

Raven's Progressive Matrices, 27, 35–36, 44, 58, 92, 99, 129; and Lynn's databases, 39, 40; and MSCEIT, 33–34; as multiple choice, 20–21, 61; popularity of, 21; and verbal similarities tests, 51, 57; and vocabulary tests, 23, 33

reaction time studies, 27–28

reading tests, 1, 6, 7–9, 23, 37, 45, 46

reciprocity, 98–99, 177n13

relationship between measures: as modest/moderate, 23, 24–25, 28, 30, 32, 33, 47–48, 72, 97, 118, 119; as nearly/almost perfect, 22, 46, 172n6; as strong/robust, 22–23, 28, 46, 97, 117, 171n7; as weak, 23–24, 25, 27, 32, 33, 36, 66, 147, 152, 153–54

repeated prisoner's dilemmas (RPDs), 88–94, 96–100, 103–6, 110, 176nn4,10

reputation, 115–16

reverse digit span, 57, 70

Ricardo, David: on law of comparative advantage, 125

Rindermann, Heiner, 118–19, 129; on cognitive ability, 7–9, 46, 47, 166, 170, 171n5

Risk, 82

Roberts, Russ, 109

Romania: average cognitive ability score in, 169; average IQ score in, 169

Rosenstone, Steven J., 128

Russia: average cognitive ability score in, 169; average IQ score in, 169

Rustichini, Aldo, 92–93, 99

Sailer, Michael, 9, 47, 170

Sala-i-Martin, Xavier: *Economic Growth*, 76–79, 130; on international capital flows, 77–79; on patience, 77–79

Sass, Tim R., 60

SAT, 3, 4, 61, 100; relationship to cooperation, 96–97

Saudi Arabia: average cognitive ability score in, 169; average IQ score in, 169

savings rate: cross-country comparisons regarding, 72–73, 80–81;

defined, 175n8; relationship to conformity, 73–74; relationship to investment, 13, 71–72, 74–76, 77–81; relationship to IQ scores, 13, 68, 71–73; relationship to patience, 71–73, 74, 75, 77–79, 84

Schmidt, Frank, 28

Schneider, Joel, 11, 40, 47–48

Scholastic Aptitude Test. *See* SAT

Schor, Juliet: on consumer spending, 74

science test scores, 5–9, 10, 46, 117

Seabright, Paul: *The Company of Strangers*, 85, 100; on cooperation, 85, 100

self-interest, 85–87, 89, 155

Shafir, Eldar: on poverty and IQ scores, 56–57; *Scarcity*, 56–57

Shamosh, Noah A., 66, 69–70

Shapiro, Jesse M., 67–68

Singapore: average cognitive ability score in, 169; average IQ score in, 72, 169; average national test scores in, 1–2, 8, 45; economic conditions in, 1–2, 8; math test scores in, 45; political conditions in, 1; savings rate in, 72, 80

Slovakia: average cognitive ability score in, 169; average IQ score in, 169

Slovenia: average cognitive ability score in, 169; average IQ score in, 169

Smith, Adam: on division of labor, 151–52; on invisible hand, 12, 86; on pin manufacturing, 151–52; *The Wealth of Nations*, 151–52

smoking, 68

Sobel, Joel: on theory of cheap talk, 147, 149–51

social feedback, 100–101
social intelligence, 32–34, 92, 94–96, 148, 149, 152
social liberalism, 129
social side effects, 124
social tolerance, 129, 136, 137
socioeconomic status, 43
South Africa: average cognitive ability score in, 9, 169; average IQ score in, 47, 72, 117, 169; da Vinci Effect in, 47; GDP per person and cognitive ability in, 9; savings rate in, 72
South Korea: average cognitive ability score in, 9, 169; average IQ score in, 45, 72, 169; GDP per person and cognitive ability in, 9; reading test scores in, 45; savings rate in, 72, 80
Spain: average cognitive ability score in, 169; average IQ score in, 72, 117, 169
Spearman, Charles: on general factor of intelligence, 18–20
standardization samples, 39–40
standardized test scores: in China, 2; in Finland, 1–2; of individuals vs. nations, 4–7; nations in top 10 percent vs. bottom 10 percent, 2; relationship to better-informed citizens, 1; relationship to cognitive skills, 2, 7; relationship to complicated negotiations, 3–4; relationship to cooperation, 1, 100; relationship to GDP per person, 7–9, 23; relationship to government corruption, 117; relationship to health, 38, 42; relationship to patient citizens, 1; relationship to peer effect, 59–60; relationship to pie-growing approach, 3–4, 100; relationship to political conditions, 1, 2; relationship to prosperity and productivity, 1–2, 5–9, 10–12, 34, 35, 39, 40, 43–44, 55, 166; relationship to success in life, 4–5; in Singapore, 1–2, 8, 45; vs. years of education, 5–7. *See also* IQ tests; literacy tests; math tests; PIRLS; PISA; reading tests; SAT; science tests; TIMSS; vocabulary tests
Stanford-Binet IQ test, 15
Star Trek III: Scotty in, 143
stereotype threat, 173n1
stockholders, 83
Strenze, Tarmo, 32
Sub-Saharan Africa: average IQ test scores in, 41–44; lead abatement in, 63; vs. United Kingdom, 42–43
Sudan, 58
Sunde, Uwe, 65–66
supply and demand, 124
Sweden: average cognitive ability score in, 169; average IQ score in, 40, 169
Switzerland: average cognitive ability score in, 169; average IQ score in, 169
Syria: average cognitive ability score in, 170; average IQ score in, 170
Syrus, Publilius: on debt, 81

Taiwan: average cognitive ability score in, 170; average IQ score in, 45, 50, 170; da Vinci Effect in, 47; economic conditions in, 45; savings rate in, 72, 80; vs. United Kingdom, 50
taxation, 108, 111, 112–13, 116, 122, 123

Telephone game, 148
Terhune, Kenneth W., 176n10
test bias, 10, 21, 25–26, 36, 39, 43, 173n1
test-taking skills, 35, 61, 62
Thailand: average cognitive ability score in, 170; average IQ score in, 170
Thompson, James, 9, 47, 170, 171n5
time inconsistency of optimal plans, 114–15
TIMSS (Trends in Mathematics and Science Study), 6, 7–9, 10, 45, 46, 47, 166, 170
tit-for-tat strategy, 89, 90–91, 98–99, 103–4, 110, 176n4
toxicology: public vs. expert opinion regarding, 121–22, 124
trade policies, 124, 125
trivia tests, 58, 123, 131
trust, 110, 113, 117; and cooperation, 88–89, 91, 92–93; trust games, 92–93, 101
Tuddenham, Read, 50
Tullock, Gordon, 128
Tunisia: average cognitive ability score in, 170; average IQ score in, 170
Turkey: average cognitive ability score in, 170; average IQ score in, 170

Ukraine: average cognitive ability score in, 170; average IQ score in, 170
unemployment, 157
unintended consequences, 124
United Arab Emirates: average cognitive ability score in, 170; average IQ score in, 72, 170; savings rate in, 72

United Kingdom: average cognitive ability score in, 170; average IQ score in, 39, 40–41, 42, 43, 48, 50, 170; da Vinci Effect in, 47; education in, 122; political attitudes and IQ in, 128–29; probability of voting and IQ scores in, 128; vs. Sub-Saharan Africa, 42–43; vs. Taiwan, 60
United States: average cognitive ability score in, 170; average IQ score in, 39, 47, 72, 170; as borrower from China, 82; da Vinci Effect in, 47; Democrats, 124, 126–27; downsizing of military, 69; economic policies, 123–24; education in, 122; GDP per person and cognitive ability in, 9; immigration to, 47–48, 159–60, 174n17; IQ and income in, 31, 32, 44; IQ and probability of voting in, 128; IQ and smoking in, 67–68; IQ scores in military, 29, 50; IQ scores of East Asians in, 45–46; lead exposure in, 63; presidential test scores, 119; Republicans, 124, 126–27; rising IQ scores in, 50; savings rate in, 72; taxation in, 122
Uruguay: average cognitive ability score in, 170; average IQ score in, 170

Vanhanen, Tatu: *IQ and the Wealth of Nations*, 38, 40–41
Veblen, Thorstein: on conspicuous consumption, 73–74; Veblen Effect, 73–74
verbal similarities tests, 51, 57
vocabulary tests, 20, 23, 33, 58, 125, 167

wages: minimum wage, 108; relationship to immigration, 47–48, 157–60; relationship to IQ scores, 4–5, 6–7, 14, 30–32, 35, 36, 43–44, 47–48, 49, 152, 153–54, 174n12; relationship to productivity, 30–31, 140–41, 144, 156

Wall Street: Gordon Gekko in, 86

Warner, John T., 69

Wechsler IQ test, 15, 20, 37, 39, 51, 125

Weede, Erich, 171n7

Weel, Jaap, 98–100

Wen Jiabao, 82

Wicherts, Jelte: on Lynn, 41–44, 56; on Sub-Saharan IQ score, 41, 42–43, 56

Wicherts, Jelte M., 173n1

Williams, Robert L., 175n18

win-stay/lose-shift strategy, 176n4

win-win outcomes, 2–3, 106–8, 109–10, 113, 151, 166

Wisconsin study of IQ and earnings, 31, 48

Wittman, Donald: on democracy and the Coase Theorem, 108; *The Myth of Democratic Failure*, 108

Wolfers, Justin, 134

Wolfinger, Raymond E., 128

Wonderlic IQ test, 176n10

Woodley, Michael A., 129

World Bank, 118

Yemen: average cognitive ability score in, 170; average IQ score in, 170

Zitzewitz, Eric, 134